RECEIVED

D0507445

NO LONGER PROPERTY OF
SEATTLE PUBLIC LIBRARY

High Heals

High Heals

HOW TWO WOMEN FOUND THEIR FOOTING IN THE MEDICAL CANNABIS INDUSTRY

Leslie Apgar, MD and Gina Dubbé

Copyright © 2019 Leslie Apgar, MD and Gina Dubbé

All rights reserved. This book or any portion thereof may not be reproduced or used in any manner whatsoever without the express written permission of the publisher except for the use of brief quotations in a book review.

ISBN: 978-1-7332267-0-7

To our family, friends, and patients

It is because of open minds and open hearts we were allowed to move forward and use cannabis as medicine to treat those suffering. We remain eternally grateful.

The most beautiful people we have known are those who have known defeat, known suffering, known struggle, known loss, and have found their way out of the depths. These persons have an appreciation, a sensitivity and an understanding of life that fills them with compassion, gentleness, and a deep loving concern. Beautiful people do not just happen.
— ELIZABETH KUBLER-ROSS

Introduction

Leslie and Gina

When you wake up in the morning, what is your first thought? Do you ever wonder, "How did I get here?" or think, "This was not the life or career that I planned"? Well, we laugh about this almost daily. "Cannabis Queen" is not the title either one of us thought we would have at this stage, or frankly, at any stage of our careers. The topsy-turvy roller coaster ride of our lives that landed us smack in the middle of the medical cannabis world was never in our master plan.

We are at the center of the "green rush"—the cannabis movement. We didn't plan on being here, but without any reservation, we can say that it is the most impactful career move and decision we have ever made.

Whatever your viewpoints are on cannabis, there is so much information (and disinformation) swirling about. This book is about the truth from our eyes: two women who own a dispensary and cannabis-product business. We can say, also without reservation, that we have seen cannabis change lives. Can you imagine having tremors so severe that you can't feed yourself? Do you take for granted the ability to hold a cup of coffee and sip it while you read your Kindle? For one of our patients, this was an impossibility. Adding the correct dose of medical cannabis to her health care regimen made all the difference. She could do the small things again— the things that we take for granted. Just being able to feed herself breakfast was a win, and her life is now forever changed.

Helping people is our passion and purpose. Leslie is a natural healer. She had the interest, curiosity, and stubbornness to persevere in a male-dominated medical world, where, to this day, men and women alike assume she is a nurse or technician instead of a doctor, strictly due to her gender. Leslie never anticipated that she would leave her medical practice after delivering thousands of babies and branch out into this fringe medicine. She further never expected this to be the most important medicine that she has ever practiced.

Gina is an entrepreneur, more comfortable in the numbers and operations of a business than with people. Her skill set is in farming new businesses—starting and growing a new enterprise—and in the cerebral chess game that is creating businesses. She never anticipated leaving the comfort of engineering and sales to start over in the cannabis space. The green rush was a perfect and fertile ground to grow a brand-new business, and she never expected the rewards of seeing people live better and die better.

We should not be friends in the traditional sense. There is hardly any common ground between us. We came from disparate backgrounds, with wildly different upbringings, educations, and experiences, yet the synchronicity of us meeting and becoming best friends, then business partners in a federally illegal enterprise has been an absolutely wild ride.

Gina's idea of medicine involves Windex and Cortaid, so she leaves the science to Leslie. Leslie cannot make any electronic device or computer work consistently, but Gina sure can. The language that Gina speaks regarding mergers and acquisitions Leslie finds a mystery. But what we do have in common is a desire to help people and make a difference. We never thought cannabis would be the way in which that was done.

We are both extremely passionate people. Leslie is all about medicine and healing, and Gina is all about creating successful business enterprises and creating cultures of kindness wherever she goes. And both of us are all about living our definition of success. You might ask yourself someday, "What is my definition of success?" We would hazard to say it's not the fancy car, fancy house, new shoes, or savings account balance. This is a fiercely personal question with answers that may evolve over time. Figuring it out early in life is an amazing bonus, if you choose to look deeply into what makes you tick, what makes you happy, what makes you fulfilled.

So we will share our story...how we woke up one morning and decided that we (a doctor and an engineer) would bid for a cannabis dispensary and a year later, remarkably win.

We decided to build the dispensary that we would like to visit. We wanted to demonstrate our vision with a clean, safe, beautiful space. A place that was discreet, unlike many of the dispensaries in operation. We wanted our consultants to be caring and compassionate and to understand that we were selling medical products, not recreational ones. We wanted a space that anyone, including our mothers, could come to for an honest and forthright discussion of cannabis. Our space has whimsical crystal chandeliers and white leather chairs—not what is typically seen in this industry.

Who do you think visits a dispensary? Do you have an image in your mind? Because interestingly, the majority of our patients are over fifty years old, and they come from all walks of life. They have been delighted by the comfortable surroundings that make them feel welcome and at home.

Fast-forward four years, and we are now the managing director and medical director of a successful and well-respected medical cannabis dispensary. We've been rated as one of *Baltimore Business Journal*'s best places to work two years running, we've launched a brand-new line of cannabis products for women called Blissiva, and we've inked a national distribution deal to make said line of products available in eleven states. Most importantly—we've helped thousands of patients find relief from their symptoms in a nontraditional way.

We are nothing if not stubborn and don't like to take no for an answer. From the outset, people in the cannabis industry would tell us, "You can't do that." But there is always a way, and we have remained true to our vision, which has always been our dispensary's motto: healing evolved, life expanded.

We have learned a tremendous amount on our journey. Some lessons were expected; some were not. Here are a few:

1. You will lose friends. Some folks can't accept cannabis as an alternative healing method and can't even agree to disagree, because of past beliefs.
2. It is harder than any other business. Many dispensary owners saw an opportunity due to the emerging market. But they aren't necessarily as business savvy as they are cannabis savvy. This makes playing in the sandbox fairly challenging.

3. Cannabis is really impactful medicine—impactful in ways that we didn't anticipate. We have helped our patients as they live and during the sad times as they died. In the following chapters, you will read about actual patients whose lives were significantly improved after they added medical cannabis to their regimens.

We learned an awful lot and continue to learn every day. In the past, we were told to "just say no" to drugs. Now we are simply encouraging others to keep an open mind. We believe cannabis is good medicine. As you read our story, you might find that you begin to think so too.

So for those of you in a cannabis-friendly state, grab your Blissiva pen. For those of you not, grab a glass of wine and settle in for a sneak peak behind the scenes of a burgeoning cannabis story, which is also the story of friendship, triumph, and change.

CHAPTER 1

Each time a woman stands up for herself,
without knowing it possibly, without
claiming it, she stands up for all women.
—MAYA ANGELOU

Leslie

Our eyes met again as we drove down the highway—neither of us could believe what we were hearing. Where did this guy get the nerve to talk to us this way?

Gina and I had scheduled a conference call after a Wednesday-evening tennis date; since we'd be together anyway—and sufficiently keyed up after a spirited round of tennis—we figured it would be a fine time for a business call. As working mothers, we relished every opportunity to streamline our schedules. What woman isn't trying to cram two things into a single time slot?

However, this call was quickly revealing itself to be an embarrassing waste of time. Neither of us could fathom what had possessed the man on the other end of the line to ask us to invest our time and money into a medical cannabis dispensary and then act as if he was doing us a huge favor.

"Can you explain your business model and when you expect to go into profitability?" Gina asked. (A reasonable question for a potential investor.)

"Oh, you wouldn't understand that," he said as he continued to mansplain. It was obvious he'd never read our bios and didn't care to know about our business successes.

I, Dr. Leslie Apgar, was and am no stranger to sexism. My business partner and best friend, Gina Dubbé, wasn't and isn't either. As a gynecologist and minimally invasive surgeon (me) and an engineer turned entrepreneur (Gina), we'd both spent much of our careers in boys' clubs. We suspected the medical cannabis industry would be yet another—and this call didn't exactly disabuse us of the notion.

This was October 2015. More than two years earlier, Governor O'Malley had signed legislation establishing a medical marijuana program, making Maryland the twenty-second state to legalize cannabis for medicinal purposes. Maryland was only now granting a limited number of licenses for growers, processors, and dispensaries, and the gentleman on the phone was putting together a proposal with a patient of mine.

I had met this patient at PuraVida, a medical spa I cofounded in 2008. I guess my modest eye for business, my laid-back West Coast attitude, and my holistic approach to medicine made me an attractive candidate for this opportunity, and I was open to it. Gina had just sold her company, TheraPearl, and was looking for a new venture; I figured I'd bring her on board as well.

"She's a venture capitalist, and this is her forte," I had told my patient. "Don't get her on the phone and waste her time, cause she's the real deal." But there we were, listening to God's gift to marijuana tell us that our legitimate business concerns were "nothing to worry about."

It wasn't a long call. As we pulled into Gina's garage, Gina looked at me, and we almost didn't have to say, "We're not gonna do this." It was clear. I was embarrassed to have wasted my friend's time and drove the half mile down to my house just shaking my head about the whole thing—but I hadn't even gotten in the door when my phone rang.

"I looked up the proposal requirements for the dispensary," Gina said. "It looks like it's twenty hours of work. So screw it. Let's just do it our damn selves."

When Gina called me to say we were going to bid by ourselves, I went through a myriad of emotions in an instant. The fact that she had the presence of mind, inclination, and courage to turn a negative experience into such an amazing opportunity is a testament to her smarts and her spirit. She was never one to shirk daunting tasks, and her confidence and decisiveness gave me courage. That willingness to jump into a new arena without proper education or training was a completely foreign concept to me. After all, I was thirty years old before I was deemed fit to practice medicine without supervision. That's a lot of school and time spent in training. I could hardly conceive that we could blindly enter this industry without anyone with experience to guide us. But you know what? Where there's a will, there's a way. Perhaps our commitment to this new endeavor was a reaction to the sexism and disregard that we had faced our whole lives. Perhaps we just snapped. Maybe we wanted the opportunity to right past wrongs or to act when in the past we hadn't. But as I reflect on the deeper drive, I believe it was more than that. We had something to say, something to contribute, and it was very personally in our voices. Gina often laughs that our approach is frequently "ready, fire, aim." This was no different. The terror I felt in my heart about putting my name, my medical license, and my reputation on the line for an alternative and relatively unproven kind of healing that my traditional medical training had disregarded—that terror was real. I wasn't entirely sure this was a good idea. But I swallowed hard, trusted my friend, and decided to jump. What the hell was I doing? I didn't even have a parachute!

Maya Angelou once said, "Each time a woman stands up for herself, without knowing it possibly, without claiming it, she stands up for all women." As half—scratch that, *more* than half—of humanity, women can't wait for anyone to give them opportunities, like that individual on the conference call; women need to *take* their opportunities. It actually seems fitting that Gina and I would get into the cannabis business at such an exciting time for both women and cannabis. The #MeToo and #TimesUp movements were changing the entire social landscape, with more women finding the courage to stand up for themselves and each other every day. Every election cycle these days sees more states legalizing cannabis. Still, there's a long way to go in both arenas; less than 5 percent of *Fortune 500* CEOs are female, and the current administration's explicit antagonism to cannabis shows that it could all fall apart at any minute.

So here we were in this changing landscape with an awesome opportunity in front of us. Sometimes it's better to not overthink things and just act. You never know what might happen until you try. That fateful day we did have the courage to try, and honestly, it has made all of the difference.

CHAPTER 2

Well-behaved women seldom make history.
— Laurel Thatcher Ulrich

Gina

OK, maybe I was too optimistic—well, no maybe about it. The proposal application for a medical cannabis dispensary wasn't 20 hours of work—it was more like 120 hours of straight writing. The proposal request was 135 pages of regulations, notices, disclaimers, instructions, forms, appendixes, and questions. Lots of questions: 185, to be exact, some of which would require several pages to answer. But the will was there, and when you have the will, you can get through even the most mind-numbing tasks as long as you make progress toward a goal. It's fair to say I was a seasoned businesswoman. I'd tackled my fair share of requests for proposals—this was just one more, though with a few key differences.

It was a lot of work, and I only had two weeks to do it. And because Leslie was off on her honeymoon in the British Virgin Islands, most of it fell to me. So one morning I put on my sweatpants, grabbed my laptop, headed to my "office" (my kitchen island—the center of our home), poured my cup of coffee, and got to work.

I should say the decision to pursue medical cannabis wasn't exactly a whim—and it certainly wasn't born of a desire to stick it to a condescending guy on a conference call. Medical cannabis fit neatly into Leslie's holistic approach to medicine, and I'd already been approached by aspiring cannabis professionals wanting me to invest in their operations. As a venture capitalist, I'm always looking for an opportunity where *disruption* occurs. And as an industry clawing its way to legitimacy after decades of operating in the shadows, cannabis is certainly one of the most significant disruptors we're going to see. The cannabis disruption, which some call the green rush, is remarkably similar to the dot-com bubble of the late nineties or the California gold rush. It's an opportunity that comes once in a generation and has the potential to affect everything around it. Times like these, if capitalized upon, provide an appropriately high reward to match the high risk. Ideas on how to capitalize had been bouncing in my head for some time. Still, there's a lot of difference between bouncing ideas and coming up with a solid plan that the Maryland Medical Cannabis Commission (MMCC) could deem acceptable.

Like much of the country, Maryland reversed course on cannabis rather quickly. In 2010, the state was number five in the nation in cannabis possession arrests. In 2014, Maryland joined the growing number of states to decriminalize cannabis or legalize it for medical use. The rollout for medical cannabis in Maryland took a long time—it was late 2015, and the state was only now getting around to accepting bids for legal growers, processors, and dispensaries.

I'd never smoked cannabis, and thanks to a thick cloud of propaganda, being poor, my security clearance (which was required for my job), and weed myths, I knew very little about it. Like any responsible mother, I'd told my kids to stay the hell away from it; up until very recently, that was all the thought I had given cannabis. If I was to give this proposal a real shot, I had to learn a lot *fast.*

The first thing I did was download six books on cannabis from Amazon. Somewhere between closing the third book and opening the fourth, I was struck by how absurd this was. If I had told my eight-year-old self that I was planning to start my own medical cannabis business, I would have had about a thousand questions for myself, the first of which would be, "What exactly is cannabis?"

■ ■ ■

I grew up in the small town of Fairmont, West Virginia, in the sixties and seventies deep in the heart of coal country. From a young age I expected—or I should say, it was expected of me—that I would be touched by the coal industry: either employed in coal myself or the wife of someone who was. One of my first memories is hearing the coal miner's report on the radio every day at 6:00 a.m., noon, and 6:00 p.m.: "Farmington number one, will work, will work, portal open." The community revolved around the mines. When the miners were working, everyone prospered. When there were union strikes, poverty reigned.

By the time I was growing up, the writing was on the wall for the West Virginia coal industry. Petroleum had already overtaken coal as the country's primary energy resource, and jobs had taken a serious dip due to ever-increasing automation. The Farmington Mine disaster—which occurred just up the road from where I lived—claimed the lives of seventy-eight miners in 1968. Still, coal was the lifeblood of the community. What could we do? People were too old or too set in their ways to change careers. And all the other ancillary businesses depended on the money that the mines generated. Nothing filled the vacuum left by the dwindling coal industry, and some people seemed to give up.

J. D. Vance describes a similar feeling of despair in his memoir, *Hillbilly Elegy*, which chronicles his upbringing in the industrial wasteland of the Rust Belt Midwest. In his introduction, he says his book is about "reacting to bad circumstances in the worst way possible. It's about a culture that increasingly encourages social decay instead of counteracting it." I cried when I read that book, because I recognized the tragic decay all too well. There is a loss of the American dream in West Virginia and many parts of this country. West Virginians and many in the US have lost faith in opportunities and upward mobility.

West Virginia shaped me in so many ways. I strive to see the positive in all people and to convey optimism, even when times are tough. Growing up, sometimes that is all you have. And that is more than most. When I fight with my impatience, I try to think about what that person is going through or fighting. It helps me bite my tongue. I keep thinking of that saying "smile and bite your tongue until it bleeds."

However, in both a positive and negative way, West Virginia has allowed me to be Teflon...I let everything slide off. I try not to even remember the bad. While it sounds good, sometimes this is *not* an admirable trait. I struggle to write this book, as I have managed to forget many of the unpleasant times of my life or points that were hard.

Compartmentalization has saved me and perhaps damaged me, but it was the only way to survive childhood and keep going. This is the core of my being and continues to define me.

Social media might not have allowed that now...but back then, it worked.

If you aren't from the area, you can't see the resignation of the people, the frustration of being caught in the region, and the history of abuse, alcoholism, and trauma. If you didn't grow up there, you don't realize that Spam is a food group, bologna sandwiches replace PB&J, and venison is a staple rather than an upscale menu option. We were "farm to table" long before it was fashionable.

But I get up every day and try to begin with a moment of gratitude. We are all lucky in some way. To be alive, to have a roof, food, family, a job, a calling...you need to concentrate on what you have versus what you don't. I try to send energy to those who are battling an illness or depression. When I look at how I grew up, that is what saves you: being grateful for what you have.

In spite of the hopelessness, I was resolved to grit it out—and grit would become the cornerstone of my life and career. I realize now that we were poor, but poverty is relative—at the time we had plenty. We thought we were just like everyone else. We played in the abandoned mines up on top of the hill until we scared ourselves. Everyone had a "party line" rotary dial phone, a black-and-white TV, and at Christmas, a tinsel tree (under which were socks and underwear).

West Virginia was a step back in time. When I was in elementary school, girls couldn't wear pants. You had to come to school in a dress or skirt, rain or shine. You could wear pants under the dress when it snowed, but you had to take them off before class. All the teachers were women, and the principal was a man. I can still remember the smell of the coal furnace (which blew up when I was in the second grade...but that's another story), Elmer's glue, construction paper, and wet wool. Counting pennies to make change or buy lunch, which was a treat. Writing cursive on lined paper. The smell of the duplicating machine's blue-ink copies.

If my parents had it their way, I wouldn't get the kind of education and career I really wanted. If I was to work at all, it would have been in a traditionally female field: secretary, teacher, or nurse. I remember my brickmason father telling me I had to take shorthand so I could support my miner husband when the mines went on strike. Though my future was always set out before me, I refused to acknowledge or accept it. At Christmas, I remember lying under the tinsel tree (which we would now refer to as "retro") and looking up through the shiny branches and wondering what it would be like in a big city. Mind you, a big city to me was most any town!

■ ■ ■

Forty-five years later, I would be sitting at the kitchen island in my home in the farm country surrounding Columbia, Maryland, clacking away at questions about medical cannabis—intellectually about as far from the coal industry as I could be.

During the two weeks up until the due date for the proposal, I got up every day at about 5:30 or 6:00 a.m. and quit around 10:00 or 11:00 p.m., taking breaks for food and my own sanity. The slow cooker bubbled while I worked so my family wouldn't starve. My parents would be proud; though I was off chasing some grand, unrealistic ambition, I still managed to put food on the table. Of course, it might take them a while to come around to the cannabis part of it.

A hundred and eighty-five questions and only two weeks to answer them. My engineer brain came up with a systematic approach: I built an evaluation criteria matrix and assigned each question a value. I'd spend the most time on the high-value questions and just steamroll through the rest. I created a special calendar to ensure I stayed on track, tackling X number of questions every day. I was fortunate to have Jamie Stowe, a tennis friend with a biology degree, to help with some of the biology and chemistry questions.

When you spend fourteen hours a day in front of a computer working on a proposal for a medical cannabis license, your mind tends to wander. I was thankful that my career had prepared me to take this on and that it wasn't wholly overwhelming. Though I'd done a lot wrong, I'd done enough right that I was in a position to make such a risky business decision. Or more accurately, I'd done enough right that I was in a position to bid for the *opportunity* to make a risky business decision.

■ ■ ■

Becoming an engineer was a long, frustrating road. I followed my instincts to get out of West Virginia, and to do that, I needed an education—preferably more than just shorthand. My parents weren't thrilled by the idea. In our traditional Italian home, the emphasis was on *men* getting an education and supporting their family. Still, we managed to compromise on West Virginia University in Morgantown, just twenty-five miles from home. Though it was so close, I'd only ever been there once or twice in my life.

I went to college thinking I would study interior design, but I switched to engineering within the first week. Interior design required serious aesthetic skill, and I didn't have it. What I *did* have were strong logic skills and grit, so engineering it was! I loved it from the first minute. Growing up in coal country, I'd seen incredible feats of engineering, and I knew engineers made good money. Unfortunately, I was woefully underprepared—particularly in the math department.

I loved college; however, my worldview was a bit different than most. My parents couldn't fund college. I worked full time and went to school full time. I was so fortunate because education was my key to freedom. I didn't realize that anyone did it any differently.

While I was taking shorthand in high school, the boys were taking trigonometry and calculus. Though I somehow managed to test into calculus once I got to WVU, it was by the skin of my teeth. Working full time, taking eighteen credit hours of classes, and trying to teach myself enough calculus to catch up to the rest of the class was a lot to ask of myself, and I failed. Seeing that F on my report card was devastating.

My parents would have been thrilled to have me back home, but I had too much grit to quit. Besides, being out of one's depth was common enough at WVU that they granted freshmen a do-over for a single class. This was the first of many do-overs I'd have in life, and I was thankful for it. This was an important lesson for me: if you have an opportunity for a do-over, take it. If there isn't one readily available, make one. We often fall into the trap of failing, and then we quit. You should not forget the lessons in why you failed, but you should use the knowledge to succeed when you try again. Some of the most important lessons are in failing and then getting up and trying again.

I'm sorry to report that not a lot of women get into engineering. This is true today, and the deficit was especially marked in the late seventies and early eighties. There were fifty male engineers for every woman in the program—I was the one with the big hair in the back row. When I went to weld, there were no gloves or equipment in my size. I ignored it, made it work, and plowed onward.

I met my husband, Dean, on a trip to the tutoring lab for help with my mechanical engineering class (Dean was my tutor). We were engaged within six months, and we got married at the end of my junior year. As there weren't two jobs for two rookie engineers in West Virginia, Dean and I applied for and got positions in the DC area. I had never been to DC—never driven on a six-lane highway, let alone one with eight lanes. It was like a bad movie about a small-town girl with big hair and a southern accent: I learned which fork to use in a restaurant, how to keep my cool when people beeped the horn at me, and how to stand up for myself.

I got a job at a company supporting avionic equipment for the US Navy and was that company's first female engineer. I took classes at the Naval Academy while working full time and earned a master's degree in engineering conferred from George Washington University.

It was hard, but I was no stranger to hard work; I preferred it. I was never bored! And my work ethic would serve me well throughout my career. I stuck with engineering for a while, worked in sales for Oracle, and eventually got on the ground floor of a computer security and research company called Trusted Information Systems. I received a substantial payout when that company was sold to McAfee, and from there I was able to step into venture capital. Everything in my career up till that point had helped me be a successful entrepreneur. From there I went into a number of businesses, and fortunately my instincts were on track more often than not. My successes allowed me to do basically whatever I wanted, and—as I'm sure that eight-year-old girl from West Virginia would struggle to understand—what I wanted was to get into the next disruptive wave in the marketplace: medical cannabis.

■ ■ ■

I'd set my mind on getting through the proposal, but I certainly felt my resolve wane as I limped through some of the more esoteric questions. *I don't need to do this*, I thought, sometime around ten o'clock one night, somewhere around question eighty-three. *Maybe I can't do this.* I knew very little about cannabis, and there were surely industry experts who allowed themselves much more time and spent hundreds of thousands of dollars on consulting fees to ensure detailed, flawless answers to every question.

I knew that feeling of insecurity all too well. I'd felt it throughout my career—that nagging suspicion that I wasn't good enough. Always hesitant to raise my hand in engineering classes in which I was the only female student, opting not to bring up a relevant point in a board meeting because I was the only blouse in a room of suits and ties. Always that feeling of not belonging—because according to my father, my mother, and everyone I knew growing up, I *didn't* belong. I was supposed to be a dutiful wife and mother, letting my husband earn the money while I stuck to the kitchen. Well, here I was in the kitchen all right—only I was putting together a proposal for a brazen new business venture, not cooking or cleaning (unless you count the slow cooker).

Throughout my career, I've always found comfort in the fact that no one really knows what they're doing. It's common for women to be unsure of ourselves because many of us have been belittled our whole lives, but there are exactly zero people who have it all figured out. Many of us act like we do, and we put our best face forward, but behind masks of steely competence are writhing snakes of insecurity.

But I grew up with grit. And that single trait is the cornerstone of all that I am. Have you taken the GRIT survey? Just look it up on the web. Simple questions, but it can fairly accurately show who you are.

Here I was, answering questions about a proposed cannabis dispensary, assuming there were industry experts out there with much better answers, much clearer visions. But eventually it dawned on me that there *was* no such thing as a cannabis industry expert. All that was needed, in my opinion, was someone with some business expertise, period. The cannabis books I read frequently contradicted each other and even themselves. The industry was (and is) so new and controversial that there simply hadn't been time to establish best practices—to see how high the weather balloon could fly. *No one knew what they were doing.* Not cultivators, not processors, not dispensary owners, not cannabis users. Even the proposal application from the MMCC was kind of a mess—a bureaucratic "cover our asses" manifesto that seemed to mistake sheer length for meticulousness. (One question was "Please describe how the licensed dispensary's hours of business will be displayed at the entrance to the public zone.")

Of course, that's the pessimistic way to look at it. The sunny side of "No one knows what they're doing" is "Anyone can step up." The moment I realized that, I felt free. Leslie and I had a vision, as naive as it was, but it was clear, concise, and cogent. Though I didn't know much about cannabis to start, I read as much as I could about it. I used my judgment to discard ideas that seemed absurd, and I used my imagination to figure out ways to do it better. I thought about what kind of dispensary I would want to visit, and I committed it to writing. I knew that Leslie would pull me back to earth if I got too carried away.

By the time Leslie came back from her honeymoon to help me finish, I felt like a wannabe Willie Nelson. I knew *a lot* more about cannabis, and I had a crystal-clear vision of how to operate a dispensary (at least my own vision—right or wrong): what kind of security system to install, what kinds of product to sell, how to display the product, how to interact with patients, and so forth. I was, however, out of my depth when it came to the medical side. Though the "Fake it till you make it" attitude works a lot of the time, medicine is best left to the folks who take twelve years out of their lives to study it (i.e., doctors). That's where Leslie came in.

■ ■ ■

Leslie and I had met a few years back when she moved into my neighborhood in Glenelg, Maryland, halfway between Baltimore and DC. Glenelg is a small town of under two thousand people: no traffic lights, two traffic circles (recent additions), and twenty minutes from a grocery store. It is bucolic and peaceful; you see a cow every now and again or a tractor on the road, and the people are really nice. The people in the community are my heroes, my inspirations, and living examples of kindness. If you are sick, the neighborhood is there. If there is a death, you are surrounded with people to cook meals, shovel snow, and cut grass. If there is a problem, you know that your posse has your back. I am eternally grateful for the friends that we made and have. Normal people. Hardworking people. Flawed people. But all were kind. And that is our credo and the credo for the dispensary: in a world where you can be anything, choose to be kind.

Leslie and my backyards were right up against each other, so when she moved in, I did the neighborly thing by bringing her an apple pie. The first thing that struck me was her height: six feet—or five feet twelve, as she would say (I'm five four, though I sometimes think I'm a foot taller). I was in awe—and her height would be the least of it, as it turned out: she was a single mom *and* a successful doctor with a great reputation. I didn't know how she did it.

At first blush, we had absolutely *nothing* in common. I grew up a West Virginia girl of modest means, and she grew up riding horses on a breezy island near Seattle, Washington. But we quickly became friends. I could see that she had a lively and interesting mind and was a truly great person. She would prove to be honest, dependable, and the kind of friend who would move the world for you. She became my rock and confidant. She made me laugh. She called me out when I was off base. It wasn't long before I realized I would do anything for her. She still makes me laugh, she still calls me out, and I love her for it.

She'd been there for me so many times that I didn't resent her going on her honeymoon. Jealous, yes (drinking margaritas on a beach sounded great), but resentful, *no*. The medical cannabis proposal was a wild whim, and she'd been planning her honeymoon for months. Also, family time and vacation are hugely important to the both of us, and there was no question that she would go and enjoy herself—she deserved it. When she got back, she put in her fair share of hours. Though I had the business side down, she was a huge asset for questions like "Please describe how the Applicant/Licensee would assure that the medical cannabis professionalism factors of experience, knowledge, and training in training dispensary agents in the sciences and use of medical cannabis would be addressed." Boy oh boy was she qualified for the job.

Leslie proofed the proposal and lent her medical/scientific expertise to the relevant questions, and we gathered everything else we needed (including five years of tax returns). The full proposal was six hundred pages in all; we spent eighty-six dollars to xerox it all, put it in green binders (a nod to the plant itself), and sent it off into the great unknown. We had no clue that more than half of the applicants had engaged professional consultants to write the proposal, and some had invested up to a quarter of a million dollars into their submissions.

We knew it would take a long time for the state to review all these six-hundred-page proposals—I learned later that more than a thousand were submitted. So we went about our lives; Leslie continued operating her med spa, and I continued enjoying my semiretirement, dipping my toes into projects every once in a while. Bidding for the dispensary license felt kind of like grabbing a dandelion seed from the air, making a wish, and letting it ride the breeze to God knows where. We worked very hard on the proposal, and we hoped we would succeed, but we didn't really expect anything. There were days I didn't think of it at all.

■ ■ ■

One year later, I received a text from a friend of mine who had seen a list of names on the MMCC's website: "Congratulations!" I was confused at first, but then it struck me.

We'd won the bid.

Oh my God—we won the bid!

Deep breath.

Wait, we won the bid?

What in the world do we do now?

Now the work could *really* begin.

CHAPTER 3

Other people will call me a rebel, but I just feel like I'm living my life and doing what I want to do. Sometimes people call that rebellion—especially when you're a woman.
— JOAN JETT

Leslie

I was in the middle of administering a bikini laser hair-removal treatment when I heard the news. Actually, I saw on my Apple Watch that Gina had texted me, and because we had been expecting to hear from the MMCC any day now, I had a pretty good idea what the text was about.

I think of myself as a caring, attentive physician, so I resisted the urge to read the text until after I was finished with the patient. Also, bikini laser hair removal isn't the kind of procedure you can discreetly excuse yourself from. It was a master class of self-control. The second the patient left, I called Gina—and when she told me that we'd won the bid, I screamed.

It was about four o'clock Friday afternoon, and my staff was happy to help me celebrate and bring in an early weekend. After the hugs and high fives, when afternoon turned to evening, I was absolutely petrified by the sheer number of unknowns ahead. I was now the attending physician for a residency program that I had to create from scratch.

You could say I'd done it before: I'd founded Pura Vida in 2008, and nearly ten years later, it was still going strong. Pura Vida was itself a bold venture when I started—some in the medical community thought I was crazy for combining women's medical concerns with cosmetic ones. But medical cannabis was a yawning void. There was so much I had to learn. Here I was, a doctor with twenty-five years of experience, someone who had already started her own business and run it for ten years, but in some ways I felt like a clueless little girl again, overwhelmed by the world. Actually, now that I think about it, I may have had more things figured out as a girl.

■ ■ ■

I enjoyed a free and privileged upbringing on Mercer Island, just outside of Seattle, Washington. I absorbed the outdoorsy spirit of the Northwest by osmosis—I learned from an early age how to swim, sail, water-ski, and pilot a boat. I hiked, camped, fished, skied, and rode bikes all over. Wide-open skies always made me feel free.

It's hard to feel any freer than when you're riding a horse. I felt utterly and completely at home in the saddle. I was fortunate enough to keep my own horses on backyard farms on the island, and I eventually moved them to nearby Kirkland, a ridiculously horsey area brimming with moneyed individuals who ride. I competed in area shows; I excelled at equitation, which is proper form while riding, and at equitation over fences, which is proper form while jumping. I was always pretty tall, which I considered a mixed blessing, but at least my long, lanky legs helped me stay on a horse better than shorter girls.

Horses taught me responsibility and accountability. While my parents made a good living, we certainly didn't have the kind of money that others in the area did. My schoolmates routinely vacationed in Hawaii during school breaks, many were given brand-new cars on their sixteenth birthdays, and as far as the equestrian world was concerned, I was competing against those with seemingly unlimited funds to purchase the best mounts, the best tack, and the best trainers.

My parents taught me to work for everything extra that I wanted, and I worked hard to support my horse habit. I quickly learned the importance of a strong work ethic, as it allowed me to pursue my true passion. I had a paper route; I awoke at a ridiculously early hour, loaded up my bike pouches and my backpack full of papers, and rode my route (many times in the rain—this was Seattle, after all). I'd dutifully retrace my territory every month with my notebook and billing sheets, trying to collect the fees, going door to door. I learned how to interact with those on my route, adjust to their specific requests, and sometimes uncomfortably ask to be paid.

I also worked at the local drugstore, Pay 'n Save, stocking, facing, stickering with an actual sticker gun, creating displays, ordering, ringing out at the registers, and all other tasks that needed to be done. Again, I learned how to interact with people—some not so nice—and I learned "The customer is always right." I also learned the importance of being accountable as my register was watched like a hawk, and I had to have numbers that matched daily or face dire consequences from management.

■ ■ ■

Fast-forward to many years later, and I've come a long way from fearing management. As nerve racking as it was to try to satisfy management, actually *being* management was a thousand times worse. And I imagined being management in a semi-illegal trade would be *ten thousand* times worse. Sometimes, fear is a gift. It is outlined in Gavin de Becker's book *The Gift of Fear*. I want to be sure that one thing is very clear: being fearless in this sense is not actually the absence of fear. It simply means being able to leverage your fear and manage it. Everyone experiences fear, and depending on who you talk to, any range of emotions can fall under fear. Anxiety, greed, jealousy, and more are fear-based emotions that affect how we act at any given time. Experiencing fear is not a bad thing. It does a lot of great things for us, and it is literally hardwired into our brains to help keep us safe.

Fear makes us more efficient—at least briefly because of the bodily changes it causes, such as the brain becoming hyperalert; the pupils dilating; breathing, blood pressure, and heart rate accelerating; and blood flow and glucose to the muscles increasing. Fear is instructive. When we experience it, we know we have something to lose and know we are pushing ourselves. We can figure out how to shift our perspective by looking carefully at our fear and where it comes from.

After the elation of the big news wore off, I spent a few minutes alone in room number 4, biting my nails. Of course, I'd thought about what kind of dispensary I'd want to operate when Gina and I were completing the proposal application, but in the year that followed, I let myself stop thinking about it. Why spend time thinking about something that might not come to pass? But now that we knew we were actually going to open a dispensary, it was time to get real.

From the outset, Gina and I knew one thing: we wanted our dispensary to be the kind of place where *we* would feel comfortable. We wanted it to be a clean, bright, comforting environment with a professional and clinical feel. Not the frightening, drawing-blood, running-some-tests type of clinical environment, but the kind of place you visit and know everything is going to be OK. We definitely did *not* want our dispensary to feel dark and dingy and, well, stoner-y—we wanted to get as far from cannabis's reputation of being an illicit drug as possible and use the space to help promote the plant as a gentle and effective medication for serious people. Because that's the truth.

Gina and I were clear about the broad strokes of our dispensary from nearly the beginning, but there were a million details to figure out—not the least of which was the practice of actually administering medical cannabis. I'd done a ton of research into this, of course, but there was still plenty to figure out. What kind of staff should we hire? What would consultation be like? How could we ensure that we received product that was consistent, effective, and convenient for patients?

What I *did* know at this point was that cannabis fit neatly into my general view of medicine. Of course, as a trained and licensed OB-GYN, I had the appropriate respect and awe for everything that Western medical science had achieved in the past decades and centuries, but I was also honest with myself about its shortcomings. Western medicine often puts Band-Aids on diseases instead of getting to the root of why people are sick. We give antibiotics for infections instead of preventing them. I was disgusted with the constant barrage of patients who wanted a pill to make them sleep, a pill to make them alert, a pill to make them happy, and a pill for their constant aches and pains. Everyone, it seemed, just wanted a quick fix instead of working to figure out why they were suffering in the first place.

When I started learning about the medicine of cannabis, a light bulb went off in my head. This is what I had been missing all those years. If cannabis helped to create balance or homeostasis in the body, the focus could be on identifying the causes and stressors that led to disease states. It appeared that cannabis allowed the body to do some serious healing and minimized the need for all kinds of pills. In med school, one of the most important lessons I learned was to constantly evaluate what meds someone is taking. Always ask if they still need them—if a lower dose could be used, and if the patient has symptoms of any kind, always consider whether one of the drugs they're ingesting is the cause. Cannabis medicine was in keeping with the kind of medicine I had always wanted to practice. The focus was on supporting wellness instead of supporting Big Pharma.

■ ■ ■

I was always fascinated by medicine, biology, and the healing process. I have horses to thank for that. In a lot of ways, they're majestic creatures, but they're not the brightest bulbs in the pack; they're easily startled and can slash and cut themselves almost anywhere. Every time the vet shows up at the farm, I can see dollar signs being flushed down the toilet.

I grew up with plenty of privileges, but again, my parents didn't have a bottomless bank account. In an attempt to defray the vet costs, I learned quickly how to treat the horses' injuries myself. The necessary hands-on and sometimes "gross" treatments I had to do didn't intimidate me, as I was highly motivated to continue with my passion. Interestingly, one of the treatments I had to do was to prevent excessive scar tissue from forming on cuts—especially on the horses' legs. Called "proud flesh" in the vet world, it's essentially an overgrowth of granulation tissue that must be alternatively cauterized with caustic powders, then treated with wet emollients to get a nice cosmetic result and to prevent loss of flexibility. I still think of "proud flesh" today as I remove scars and other imperfections from my Pura Vida patients.

I always thought I'd go into veterinary medicine and likely focus on horses and other large animals. I figured this would afford me a certain income that would allow me to continue riding. This was an entirely realistic goal—unlike with Gina's childhood expectations, college was a given for me (yes, even for young women), and honestly, grad school was an assumption as well.

I had a terrible time in high school, though the education aspect of it was excellent. Socially, I didn't feel that I fit in, so I focused on schoolwork and endured until graduation. My favorite class, embryogenetics, taught by Mr. Tougaw, cemented my passion for biology and medicine. There, we made paraffin-embedded tissue slides and stained them at various stages of chicken embryonic development (like I said, excellent). Mr. Tougaw was a profoundly cool guy who pushed boundaries and forced us to think outside of the box. He introduced us to some fairly big concepts, one of which I still remember: "What does everything have in common with everything else?" The answer was space. The concept was that we are mostly space, with infinitesimally small particles that make up atoms, matter, and form, but the space in between is utterly vast, and space unites every single thing in the universe.

Speaking of space—I needed some. Lots of my peers went to the University of Washington, just fifteen minutes away in Seattle. Desperate for a change of scenery, I instead decided on Washington State University, clear on the other side of the state in Pullman. They also happened to have one of the best veterinary programs in the country at the time. True, WSU's undergrad reputation was somewhat lacking, but I didn't want the immediate debt of an out-of-state school, and honestly, I didn't want to try that hard. Though my mom did talk me into enrolling in the honors college, for which I would end up being very thankful.

I majored in zoology, as I thought I would pursue veterinary medicine, but I quickly realized a few things. First, the pre-vet students weren't the most social. In fact, they weren't approachable at all. Were these my people? It certainly didn't appear so. Second, I obviously loved animals *way* more than people. This was a problem, as my tender heart couldn't deal with the animals in pain or with owners who simply didn't want to deal with their pets anymore and brought them in to be put down. Nope. Not for me. Third, vet school was super competitive, and I wasn't sure I would make the income necessary to pay back my loans.

So human medicine it was. I aligned myself with the premed club and followed the rubric necessary to get the prerequisites completed. But I felt exhausted by the time I earned my degree, and I was in no rush to repeat many of the grad school–level classes I had just taken. So I took a much-needed year off and worked for an internal medicine group in Seattle while I cemented my decision to go to med school.

I was able to take some pretty transformative classes during that year that taught me a lot about myself and my innermost motivations. It's scary to look inside yourself and be vulnerable. You might not like what you see. But once you're armed with this information, you can use it in constructive ways instead of destructive ones. The lessons I learned during this year have stayed with me even to this day: how to create win-win solutions, how to understand the ego, and how to temper my "need to be right," my need for perfectionism, my fear of failure, and the like. When I acknowledge truths about myself, I'm able to negotiate my path forward better with the self-deprecation and humor that make everything so much more fun and make life much more productive.

When I deemed myself ready, I applied to medical school. At the time, the University of Washington was the only medical school available for Washington, Alaska, Montana, and Idaho. All the kids in those states were applying to UW, and competition was fierce. My MCATs were OK but not great—I figured it was just a number, and it didn't *really* have much to do with my success as a doctor. UW did not agree, and I did not get in to their med school.

Wow. I was devastated. This was a pretty huge failure for me, and it was terrifying. Failure wasn't necessarily something I was familiar with, and I had a hard time pulling myself out of a depressive funk and figuring out a new course.

Fortunately, I got accepted at a few different schools throughout the country. Penn State was my top choice, as I had family in Pennsylvania and would at least have some sort of security blanket available to me. I pulled myself off the ground and signed the financial aid forms for PSU. Now I would have to move away from all that was familiar and go to the East Coast.

Talk about culture shock. Central Pennsylvania was devoid of the tall mountains I'd known my whole life. Healthy food options were few and far between. Proudly displayed in the hospital cafeteria was the label "Lard added for flavor." The culture felt so very different from what I'd known: very closed, stiff, and formal. I remember being chastised for calling a patient by her first name instead of "Mrs. So-and-So." To me, the formality between doctor (or student) and patient was a barrier, and it didn't resonate with me. Healing happens best when there is a balanced interaction, and I fought to stay who I was and be sincere with the patients whenever possible.

The school side of things got a lot more fun once we started with the rotations throughout the specialties, and I really considered plastic surgery as a career. For those who don't know, surgery is the epitome of the boys' club. It's still male dominated, even today, and the hours are intense. I curse like a sailor, and I always thought that I could hang with the guys in any situation, but when I would walk into the operating room, the guys would stop talking midconversation. For one of the first times in my life, I really felt my sex. I was treated differently because I was female.

To embark on a surgical residency was quite an undertaking, but to fight my sex every step of the way just seemed untenable. Obstetrics and gynecology, while still a surgical residency, celebrated women and in fact came with a reverse discrimination *toward* women, as female patients were increasingly wanting to see female practitioners. This was the compromise I decided on, and I have no regrets.

What followed was a grueling few years of residency filled with many 3:00 a.m. calls and thirty-six-hour shifts. They say there's never a good time to start a family, so I got married to a fellow OB-GYN with blue eyes and a motorcycle, and together we had a beautiful daughter, Alexa. It would all prove too much to handle, and our marriage crumbled right at the end of our residency—before it could even really begin, in my view. It was a heartbreaking time, but like with my horses, I had to excise the "proud flesh": I couldn't let a bit of scar tissue slow me down.

My daughter and I moved to Maryland, where I joined an all-women's OB-GYN practice. My mother moved from Arizona to help me through those dark times, my daughter was growing up to be a thoughtful and self-reliant young woman, and I had great support from friends and colleagues. One of my partners even had horses that she let me ride. Still, taking on the responsibility of a high-stress job and single motherhood was *tough*.

Gina had perhaps the greatest impact on helping me heal—Gina and her delicious apple pie. She would dismiss that pie as just a common neighborly courtesy, but it was a lot more than that. It was the first of a thousand generosities, including feeding my kid breakfast and putting her on the bus when I was called into work.

She was also an inspiration to me: she and her husband worked full-time jobs and had two fantastic kids. They had no nanny and no magic wands lying around that I could see, yet she still had the time and the inclination to cook and to bake. She was so freaking smart, and somehow she just seemed to have her shit together in a way that I did not. We were absolute and complete opposites, so of course we became best friends. Our utter amusement at each other's take on life was and still is a constant source of hilarity. We are fiercely protective of each other, and I know we would lie down in the street for each other.

Gina helped give me the courage to found Pura Vida in 2008. A med spa always seemed like an attractive concept—and a much-needed one. My patients asked me repeatedly to look at their skin, take off unsightly moles, or use a laser to remove their unwanted hair. They wanted the "Pap and wax" treatment: many would half-jokingly say to me, "While you're down there and all..." They were persistent, and I started listening. Then one of my partners and I decided to open a medical spa separate from our OB-GYN practice. "Just do it," Gina told me. "You'll do great." She used to come over, and we would take turns microderming each other's faces in my kitchen while drinking wine and giggling over the insanity of our lives.

■ ■ ■

We had no idea what insanity was. Nearly ten years later, we would be out together celebrating our successful medical cannabis dispensary bid with two bottles of champagne—enjoying the moment but also steeling our nerves against the mountain of hard work to come.

Our dispensary, which existed only in our minds and in a long bureaucratic document, would become real. But there were a lot of steps between then and now. The first one was to actually find a space for it.

Mr. Tougaw told me that space is the one thing we all have in common. Unfortunately, cannabis was still too controversial for many real estate owners in Maryland: no one wanted to rent, lease, sell or share their space with us.

CHAPTER 4

A woman is like a tea bag—you never know
how strong she is until she gets in hot water.
— ELEANOR ROOSEVELT

Gina

The condominium board had already come to a decision: they didn't want us there. From the moment we walked in—pretty binders in hand, presentation ready, and frequently asked questions printed—and took a seat, we could tell that this wasn't going to be the place for our dispensary. They let us talk, but they had made the decision prior to our arrival. And that's the way that it was and is with cannabis: the old viewpoints and stigma just didn't allow for open minds.

We were in our sixth month of looking for real estate for our dispensary, and we were quickly going into desperation mode. We picked this condo building in a location that wasn't our first choice. Still, we figured we ought to give it a shot, as time was a-wasting, and we felt like we were running out of shots.

We knew what their decision would be, but we went through with the presentation anyway. We gave them a full rundown of how we planned to operate the dispensary. We presented them with our credentials. We even made the compelling point that our security system—a state-mandated requirement—would make the whole building safer. But the stone-cold faces on the eight men and one woman said it all: it was a no go.

■ ■ ■

The failure with the condominium board was disappointing, but it was hardly surprising. Over the past six months, we'd already come down so far from the thrilling high of having our bid accepted—it was hard to imagine getting much lower. Nothing was going as planned.

We hit hurdles right out of the gate: even before we could find a place to set up shop, we knew we had to secure banking. Unfortunately, my bank, like the condominium board, didn't want anything to do with us.

To understand the conflict between banking and the cannabis industry, you need to understand how banking works in this country. The Federal Reserve has the authority to audit, supervise, and regulate US banks as a compromise between private enterprise and government regulation. The US government also classifies cannabis as a Schedule I drug on par with heroin and cocaine. Eighty years ago, the federal government banned the sale, cultivation, and use of cannabis, and that prohibition remains intact at the federal level. This creates serious issues for the cannabis business; the federal government has essentially banned banks and credit unions from accepting money made in an illegal industry.

That said, the US Treasury and Justice Department have stated—at the time of this writing at least—they won't go after institutions that keep a close eye on clients who conduct state-approved legal business. But that's not a law; it's a statement that could be rescinded at any moment and overruled by an administration instituting new laws.

Given this uneasy reality, banks tend to be cautious about the cannabis industry. My bank, which I'd done business with for thirty-five years, must have seen in the paper that I'd won the medical cannabis dispensary bid. Not more than a month after, the branch manager called and "invited" me to remove all my accounts from the bank. Wow, what a surprising call. It was a cold slap in the face—my husband and I had our mortgages there, all our checking accounts, our kids' savings accounts.

Leslie and I knew that going into the cannabis business would have some consequences, but I hadn't expected this. The risk was compounded by the fact that the business, at this point, was in my name: Gina Dubbé. If I'd had my druthers, I would have submitted the dispensary bid under an LLC or a nom de business, like Elizabeth Arden, but Leslie and I had acted so quickly that there was no time.

Now, I had no desire to hide the fact that I was in the cannabis business, but discretion can be a virtue, and it's nice to keep your personal life and business life separate. The fact that all my associates could see "Gina Dubbé" and "cannabis" in the same sentence would bring about unpleasant consequences—one of the first of which was my bank's decision to cut ties.

Again, given the tension between federal banking oversight and the government's view on cannabis, it's understandable that a bank would be overly cautious. But something seemed off about the bank's offer. I asked them, "Wait a second—are you asking any of the men to leave the bank?" I hadn't been in the cannabis business for long, but I'd been around long enough to know that many of my male associates were still happily banking with their personal banks of choice—including this one. I wasn't going to give up so easily. I told them, "When you ask them to withdraw their accounts, then you can ask me, but until then, no."

If it were only about the cannabis business itself, maybe I could have understood where they were coming from—but I couldn't help feeling like I was being singled out because I was a woman. Call it instinct. Any woman reading this has probably encountered this: sometimes our exclusion or lack of opportunity is explicit, as in "Ladies not permitted," but more often it's subtle and barely perceptible. I'd spent my career in male-dominated fields, and I knew what it felt like to be talked down to and dismissed by men. If this bank snafu had happened earlier in my career, I might have thought, "Oh no, the bank wants me to withdraw my accounts—I suppose I better do it." But one of the great discoveries of my career has been that *I can push back. I need to do this for the women who will follow.* I didn't believe they had a good enough reason, so I dug in my high heels.

Our great institutions have been built around the needs of, primarily, men. There've been some critical strides in the last century to correct this, but one century can't unseat the foundations of our great institutions—or established ways of thinking. So many women are content to go with the flow because they don't even realize they're being denied something. I'll admit I was one of them. Just like so many of us enjoy privileges we aren't even aware of, those of us without certain privileges often don't realize we're being treated unfairly, as it's the only life we've ever known. Learning to spot unfairness takes time and keen observation, but if enough of us call it out, things can change.

Sure enough, things changed: after I pushed back, the bank stood down, and I got to keep my personal accounts. So at least we weren't going *backward*, but the fact remained that we needed a banking partner for our dispensary, and I knew the prospect was a solid no for my bank.

The whole ordeal was the first notice—before our friends, before the community—that we were treading in uncharted waters. Cannabis was going to be a tough sell, especially cannabis sold by women. But we'd always prided ourselves in being upstanding, honest, good citizens, and we took comfort in that—and in the fact that we were doing this together.

At the end of the day, we had the law on our side: not federal law, mind you, but *state* law, and that's not nothing. And since Maryland had just legalized medical cannabis dispensaries, some banks *had* decided to get in the game. I caught wind of a bank based wholly in Maryland that had decided to fund a finite number of cannabis businesses. We reached out to them, and they would turn out to be excellent partners. They don't have a lot of clients, so they make a lot on fees, but we're incredibly grateful to have them and have a wonderful working relationship with someone at that bank. Maryland is lucky in that regard; some states have no banks that can handle it. Here's hoping we get a safe national banking system for cannabis someday soon.

■ ■ ■

With banking squared away, we turned our attention to finding space. We suffered plenty of rejection well before our meeting with the condominium board; right away we encountered that familiar refusal to conduct business with a cannabis-related venture. Many of the buildings we looked at were owned by companies that weren't open to the idea, either because they operated in multiple states or because they flat-out didn't want us. Still, we knew where we wanted our dispensary to be, and we were determined to get in.

Back when we submitted our bid, we got to select our top choices for which Maryland legislative district would host our dispensary. Since our bid's score was so high, we got our first choice: district 12 (yes, just like the Hunger Games). Everywhere within the district was an easy commute for us, and as a mostly urban district, there'd be no shortage of clients.

Of course, finding a place in district 12 came with some challenges. For one, it's an oddly shaped district (like so many are, thanks to gerrymandering). It's a zigzag mess that stretches west to east from Columbia, Maryland, to Baltimore, with one section as narrow as one or two city blocks. A few times our realtor presented us places that were outside of district 12, which of course weren't going to work. But we didn't blame him; it's tough to make sense of it when one building is in district 12 and the building across the street isn't.

Early on, we had our sights set on an abandoned bank. Banks are usually housed in nice, roomy buildings, and we figured the vault would elegantly satisfy our state-mandated security needs. Plus, it would have been a nice twist of irony to run our dispensary out of an old bank—that's one way to get a bank involved in the cannabis industry.

Unfortunately, we were thwarted by the area's real estate investment trusts (REITs). REITs are often publicly traded and federally funded companies that own income-producing real estate (including banks). And because the ones we were dealing with were federally funded, their hands were tied by that pesky "Cannabis is illegal under the federal guidelines" thing. And here's the kicker: if any of their lessees are found to conduct federally illegal activity, the government has justification to raid *the entire building*—not just the space with the alleged illegal activity. Renting to us was too big a risk, and they were unwilling to sell properties to us either. Because REITs owned seven abandoned banks and all the big shopping plazas we wanted to get into, this made life very difficult. By the way, all seven of those banks are *still* abandoned as of this writing. Is an abandoned bank really more appealing than a medical cannabis dispensary?

Unfortunately, many folks thought so. Our realtor would show us a property, and the property owner would back out. We'd talk to a condominium board, and they'd show us the door. Basically, any building that held a bank note on it wasn't in the cards, as the banks feared that renting to a cannabis business would lead to foreclosure. That combined with public sentiment and worry made us outcasts. And really, I can't fault people for being concerned; it makes sense that folks would worry that something they don't understand (especially something that has just been legalized and is typically thought of as an addictive recreational drug) would somehow spoil where they lived.

Our bid was accepted in December 2016, and in July 2017 we were still looking for property that was up to our standards and, you know, actually possible for us to lease or buy. But that's when we finally hit a break, thanks to one of Leslie's patients. She said, "Have you thought of Dr. Ross's facility? He has a medical arts building, and he does holistic medicine—this kind of thing is totally his speed."

Leslie knew his name, called him up out of the blue, and laid it all out for him. He said, "You know what? I think I have something that might work. Why don't you and Gina come on by?"

Long story short, this was our place. We fit in well with the other tenants in the building—including a physical therapist, a naturopath, and an apothecary. Our morals and ethics were the same, and together we created a mutually beneficial healing community. Plus, we were thrilled to inhabit a building that already had a patient population.

The only thing was that our security needs (i.e., a heavy vault) meant that our dispensary had to be on the ground floor, and the only space available in Dr. Ross's building was on the second floor. But Dr. Ross, in a stunning display of generosity, offered to move his own med spa into the upstairs space so we could move into the ground floor space. After such a long streak of bad luck, we couldn't believe our good fortune.

Helen Mirren, in a commencement speech to Tulane University in 2017, said, "The trick is to listen to your instinct, grab the opportunity when it presents itself, and then give it your all. You will stumble and fall, you will experience both disaster and triumph, sometimes in the same day, but it's really important to remember that like a hangover, neither triumphs nor disasters last forever. They both pass and a new day arrives. Just try to make that new day count."

We definitely had some stumbles, maybe a fall or two, and perhaps even "work hangovers" during this time, but we were still grabbing the opportunity and ready to make our new day count—and make it count we did.

While we were disappointed that it took so long to secure a space, we were still grateful for the process. It helped us understand just what we were up against in our uphill battle of opening a medical cannabis dispensary—and a successful one at that.

Long after we secured our space, I found myself thinking about that meeting with the condominium board. Though we essentially walked in knowing that they wouldn't let us lease their space, I was heartened that they had agreed to the meeting in the first place. It meant that at least one of the board members was open to the idea of medical cannabis, and perhaps the others were open to changing their minds. If we had tried something similar just five years earlier, we'd have been laughed out of the room—or perhaps even escorted off the property by the police, as it was illegal then. But enough minds had changed within the previous five years to allow for the legalization of cannabis in Maryland, and we were hopeful that more minds would change in the coming months and years: especially once they saw what Leslie and I had in store.

■ ■ ■

Of course, our dispensary wasn't going to change anyone's minds if no one knew what to call it. So Leslie, me, and our marketing expert, Kait LeDonne, got together one evening, opened a bottle of wine, and brainstormed name ideas. We had our laptops open too—this being the digital age, we knew that whatever name we chose also had to have an available domain.

Because our whole mission involved getting people to take medical cannabis more seriously, we knew we had to stay away from silly and overly punny names, as fun as they are. So "Royal Highness" and "Best Buds" were out. Still, we wanted to make it clear that we were indeed a medical cannabis dispensary. We came up with the mantra "Healing evolved, life expanded," and from there we landed on "Greenhouse Wellness." It had a fresh, natural, welcoming sound to it, and it hit all the points we set out to hit.

A bank, a space, and a name: we were well on our way to opening a dispensary. Now we just needed people to help run it.

CHAPTER 5

I'm tough, I'm ambitious, and I know exactly
what I want. If that makes me a bitch, okay.

— MADONNA

Leslie

Diana was a small thing—maybe five feet two—and her husband, Jeff, had that weary, determined look of someone engaged in a long battle. Like many of the patients who came in for medical cannabis consultations, they had an air of frustration and desperation. They had been looking for an option dealing with medical cannabis for a long time. One harmful assumption about medical cannabis is that all the "patients" are really just stoners looking for a quick legal fix; in Diana and Jeff's case, this couldn't be further from the truth.

Diana's husband had been diagnosed with lung cancer twice and beat it back twice, and now he was battling it a third time. This time they had elected to try nontraditional treatment for a variety of reasons, one of which was because the cancer had spread to his brain.

Though Maryland had approved medical cannabis, the product itself was not yet available for legal public consumption. Still, Diana had the courage to find a whole pound of the (still technically illegal) cannabis that *was* available on the illicit market. A pound may not sound like a lot, but we're talking about cannabis: that's basically enough to fill a pillowcase, and it certainly wasn't cheap. But she needed that amount to prepare the cannabis medication known as Rick Simpson's Oil, named after a Canadian medical cannabis activist. Through great personal risk and effort, she underwent the complicated process of preparing the oil in her home. Fortunately, the prying eyes of her neighbors weren't too prying, or perhaps they didn't mind, and Diana was able to treat her husband. It was so very impressive. We were happy to help fill in the gaps in her research and get her husband the treatment he needed, but that wasn't all: we could tell she had the kind of drive and motivation we wanted in our staff. On the intake form Diana had filled out for her husband, where she'd outlined her experience thus far with cannabis, Gina wrote, "Need to hire her."

■ ■ ■

Diana was one of the first of a series of highly qualified and talented members of our staff, and staffing Greenhouse Wellness with such people was a vital part of our vision. But before we hired Diana—before we hired anyone—we had to make sure the space itself was ready.

After Dr. Ross had generously granted us space in his building (not just any space—*his* space), we had quickly gotten to work building it out the way we wanted it. Gina and I had done a lot of research into cannabis dispensaries from around the country, and we knew the kind of dispensary folks expected: dim lighting, hand-drawn signs, large jars of flower on the counter, and pretty rows of ornate pipes and other "pieces" beneath glass cases. That was totally fine for the recreational crowd, of course, to accommodate what a certain customer base expects, but we didn't like how this setup supported the popular perception of cannabis. We thought our patients—many of whom were only just coming around to the possibility that cannabis is useful for more than getting high—would be intimidated or even put off by having certain cannabis stereotypes thrown into their faces.

From the beginning, Gina and I knew we wanted to take a new approach. Our guiding principle was "Let's make this the kind of dispensary we'd visit," or even "Let's make this the kind of dispensary our *parents* would visit." Though my family was all on board with Greenhouse Wellness and very supportive, Gina's family—particularly her parents—was not comfortable with the entire concept. We figured if Gina's parents could feel comfortable in our dispensary, we'd call it a success.

We envisioned a clean, bright, safe, and comforting setting. One of our sources of inspiration was the Apple Store, where everything looks smooth, efficient, intentional, and welcoming. We knew we didn't want an armed security guard at the door, as many other dispensaries had, nor did we want a metal detector. We felt those things would contribute to a miasma of fear, suggesting that this was a place where you might get robbed or otherwise be in danger. Though we understood why other dispensaries would take these measures, we felt it fit right into the cannabis critics' narrative—that this is a dangerous drug that should be illegal.

Instead, we built out the space to be as open and welcoming and accessible as possible. We opted for a white interior with white leather seating and warm hardwood floors. Clear glass tabletops and clear glass vases with bright, cheerful flowers. Elegant crystal chandeliers dangling above a quartz countertop. Brightly colored stools for patients to sit on (or to move aside for the sake of their walkers or wheelchairs). Large touchscreen monitors on which patients could browse products at their leisure. Discreet consultation rooms for patients who wished to discuss their medical needs in private. And all of it was bathed in natural light, which was a big deal for us.

If you've ever been to a cannabis dispensary, you know that natural light isn't that common—most others prefer blacked-out windows or windowless spaces. There's a reason for this: thanks to the national credit card companies' unwillingness to process cannabis transactions, dispensaries have to be cash only. This, combined with the product's desirability, makes dispensaries potential targets for thieves—and windows are, well, breakable. We may have been naive about some things in the early stages, but we did our due diligence here: to ensure both natural light and sufficient security, we opted for bulletproof glass.

In that same vein, we were required to maintain tight control over who came into our dispensary—but instead of hiring an armed security guard and giving our entrance a "prison visiting hours" vibe, we created a spacious waiting room with a registration area where people could register as patients. Many scoffed at our vision for a cannabis dispensary, nudging us toward the traditional space where a lifelong cannabis user might feel more comfortable, but we stayed true to our instincts, and that made all the difference.

■ ■ ■

As great as it is to have a warm, welcoming, and safe cannabis dispensary, it wouldn't mean much without kind, capable, and professional people to staff it. Everyone that we hire is kind and will go the extra mile, will take the extra minute. A lady came into the dispensary, and Suzanne, one of our amazing consultants, worked with her for nearly an hour. She had been told a number of things at other dispensaries that were not right and were not working for her. After she was done, Suz walked her to the door and gave her a hug. A small, gentle gesture. The woman had tears in her eyes. Thanks, Suz, for being you and seeing that she needed the kindness. It costs nothing but means so much.

To us, Diana (and Suzanne and all of our consultants) embodied the kind of people we wanted to work at Greenhouse Wellness: smart, compassionate, driven, and knowledgeable about the medical benefits of cannabis. Diana came in looking for medical advice for her husband, and she left with medical advice *and* a job.

From the outset, Gina and I knew we wanted nurses on our staff. After all, we were selling medicine—and who better to dispense medicine than medical professionals? Though nurses command a higher salary, you get what you pay for: these are people who by virtue of their training and experience have come to understand a thousand little philosophies about health and health care. They have the compassion, patience, and fortitude necessary to speak with patients—some of whom are heartbreakingly sick—and make sound medical recommendations.

In researching existing dispensaries, we noticed that many hired employees based on their expertise with cannabis. This is, of course, a perfectly reasonable thing to do. However, considering that cannabis was up until this point illegal, many of these cannabis experts had operated, by necessity, in a world of illicit commerce. While we have known many perfectly capable cannabis dispensary employees, a disproportionate number of them are people who had previously been more or less unhireable—in part because of their unhealthy cannabis habits or their proclivity for nonmedical use. To put it less politely, many dispensaries gravitated toward stoners who they could pay minimum wage.

But with our focus on medicine, it made sense to hire staff members with medical experience, cannabis experience, or advanced degrees in fitness, biology, or chemistry, and we didn't mind paying a little extra to get the kind of expertise we wanted and needed for Greenhouse Wellness. That said, most of us have encountered medical professionals who are a little less than warm, shall we say. What we loved about Diana, and what we came to look for in our employees, was *kindness*. "Hire the personality, train the skill" has become my motto for staffing.

We knew that patients would be taking a huge personal risk by coming to see us—combating their own prejudices toward cannabis, risking judgment from their friends and loved ones, divulging personal information about their health. For these patients, who were often scared, desperate, and out of options, visiting our dispensary was a trust fall—we wanted to be sure that we had staff members in place to catch them. We set out to provide real patients with real medicine, and to do that, we needed real medical professionals.

■ ■ ■

Of course, we could hire a hundred nurses, and there would still be a legion of doctors doubtful that cannabis could be a viable alternative medicine. Hell, I earned plenty of scoffs from fellow doctors when I left my OB-GYN practice to focus full time on my med spa, Pura Vida—which in their eyes must have looked like a five-star hospital compared to a medical cannabis dispensary.

The thing is, doctors go through hell to become doctors: after earning a four-year bachelor's degree, they attend four years of medical school, then three to seven years of residency (or longer, depending on the specialization). After a doctor goes through that much school and training, they might start thinking they know everything. They place a lot of trust in their knowledge and training because when they learn it, it's the latest in medical science. But the beautiful thing about medicine is that it's often changing—something you learn in the first year of medical school could change by the time you graduate, and it could be completely debunked by the time you complete your residency. This constant change and improvement of medical science is the reason why we no longer talk of humors or recommend bloodletting.

When I left my OB-GYN clinic to focus on the intersection between women's health and cosmetics, some of my colleagues saw it as kind of a betrayal to the sacred practice of medicine. Instead, I saw it as filling an unfilled niche: using minimally invasive procedures to address cosmetic issues that affected my patients' mental and physical wellness.

It was also—and this is important—what I really wanted to do with my career. Though some former colleagues expressed their distaste for Pura Vida behind my back (and to my face), I knew I was being true to myself. And though there were (and are) plenty of naysayers, being impeccably and authentically myself is the best thing I can be. What other people think is more their problem than mine, and frankly, it's none of my business.

To flip the status quo and challenge our beliefs, we have to start with curiosity and a questioning of why the default exists. Most people are familiar with the concept of déjà vu, the idea that we have already experienced something. The other side of the coin is vuja de, experiencing something you know that you've seen before that feels fresh and new, bringing about a new perspective. Like ours on cannabis.

I carried this attitude to Pura Vida and now to Greenhouse Wellness. My medical mind was open enough to embrace cannabis as viable medicine, and starting a medical cannabis dispensary was what I wanted to do. If my medical colleagues were upset by my decision to start Pura Vida, they were freaking out about Greenhouse Wellness.

Still, I had been around long enough to trust my instincts. I had the same education, the same training, the same experience as countless other doctors—why should I assume they know better than me? In fact, I could argue that my willingness to bring new evidence into my personal philosophy of medicine made me an even *better* health care provider. When self-doubt creeps in, which is all the damn time, I try to remember that.

I didn't get into medical cannabis because I thought it was edgy or because I thought it would make me exceptionally rich—I got into it because I believed it could be effective medicine.

Our bodies already make chemicals similar to the cannabinoids in cannabis and that control or help modulate a number of systems in the body, including those related to immunity, inflammation, appetite, and pain. The substances produced in our own bodies, called endocannabinoids, are produced on demand and quickly metabolized. They're intimately involved in our most primitive nervous system, the endocannabinoid system.

These cannabinoids react with similar chemicals in your body to reduce anxiety, reduce inflammation, alleviate nausea and vomiting, improve appetite, and relax muscles. Despite the lack of formal studies done in the US (yet another impediment imposed by the federal government), I had seen what cannabis could do to alleviate the symptoms mentioned above and many others. And much of it was done through self-medication and guesswork—I got excited thinking about the potential for cannabis doled out by a medical professional who understands the chemical processes of medicine in the body.

Though I felt I had a better grasp on cannabis as medicine than most others operating cannabis dispensaries in Maryland, I knew there was still much to learn. Part of the reason many doctors are skeptical of cannabis is because they just don't know anything about it—and since they don't know anything about it, they might assume it's not worth knowing about. But I think curiosity is a beautiful thing: it caused me to learn, learn, learn; read, read, read; ask questions; and go to courses. And because of all that, I became comfortable and confident helping people navigate medical cannabis, be they our employees or our patients.

■ ■ ■

Long after we hired Diana, her husband, Jeff, would beat back cancer for the third time—even though it had spread to his brain, and his doctors had sent him home. I can't say for certain how instrumental our advice was in curing the disease, but I know it brought him crucial relief from his symptoms, improving his headspace and overall health as his other medications did their work.

Diana and Jeff likely wouldn't have even come to us if they hadn't caught wind of a medical cannabis dispensary that *actually focused on medicine*. And they wouldn't have wind of us if we hadn't started cobbling together a reputation as a clean, safe, welcoming place for patients looking for safe and effective alternative medicine.

Diana was among the first hires who would turn out to be a bona fide team member. In some ways, she was the mold we used to shape others. Greenhouse Wellness quickly became a smooth-operating, self-sustaining machine: we had a chief resident who could train the next resident until our staff was everything we dreamed of. And apparently the feeling was mutual—we would later become the first dispensary to be nominated for and win a "Best Workplace" award from the *Baltimore Business Journal*. That, together with an impressively low staff turnover rate, tells me we're on the right track.

■ ■ ■

Unfortunately, advice was all we could offer Diana and Jeff at the time of their consultation, as we had no product. We had the space, the knowledge, and good people on our staff—we were prepared to begin providing medicine to patients, but Maryland wasn't. The state's rollout of its medical cannabis program was moving at a glacial pace: the legislation was signed by the governor in April 2014, but the licenses were not awarded for processors, growers, and dispensaries until 2016. And here we were, deep into 2017 with no actual product to sell.

And even when the product became available, it was still difficult to get the kind of product we wanted in the volume we wanted for the price we wanted. Every new industry is bound to have some growing pains—and once this industry got going, it started growing like, well, a weed.

CHAPTER 6

> The higher the better, it's more about an
> attitude. High heels empower women in a way.
> — CHRISTIAN LOUBOUTIN

Gina

"I understand that a dispensary down the street from us purchased
your product for twenty dollars a gram. Can I ask why you're offering us forty dollars a gram?" I uncrossed my free arm and reflexively
put my hand on my hip. The man on the other line couldn't see this
power stance, obviously, but I stuck with it anyway. This was one of
many phone calls I made to growers, doing the hard work of chasing
down the best prices for our product.

"We can't charge you that price," said the voice on the other
line.

I was taken aback by the clipped response but had no trouble
reciprocating his curtness. "Why not?"

"Because that price was for a certain volume."

In any business, it's of course good practice to give discounts for bulk purchases—but 50 percent? That seemed excessive to me. They couldn't have purchased *that* much more volume than us. Still, I couldn't say I was completely surprised.

When growers come out with flower, they set the pricing. Some post prices on trade websites and exchange it, and you can see their products advertised, but then some don't. Some people—both growers and processors—sell to who they want to sell to. Now, of course, this happens in every type of business—relationships impact your pricing, as does the quantity and volume that you buy. In *many* industries, there are little groups here and there that only like to do business with each other. There are a number of reasons someone may want to work only with friends and well-known colleagues, and some are absolutely legitimate. But some reasons are also just excuses for cronyism, which can turn into the worst type of good ol' boys' clubs. And this often results in sweetheart deals for some and sour deals for anyone who isn't part of the club.

"If we purchased that volume, would you lower the price to twenty dollars a gram?" I'd been through this before. He would find some excuse not to sell to us at that price—maybe claim to be too low on product to be able to sell such a volume at this time. Still, I had to ask.

Pretty much out of the gate, Leslie and I were questioned and challenged regarding what we wanted to stock, what we wanted to offer our clients, and even how we were going to package it. For every blatant challenge to our way of doing business, there are a dozen almost unperceivable slights and exclusions—even now. At times it's clear that we're deliberately excluded from knowledge of exotic or highly desired strains, and we often aren't privy to other intricacies of the cannabis industry due to our relationship with others in the industry and how we're perceived. We have to do it all the hard way.

As women in *many* other industries can attest, it's not an easy thing to be in a field where the mere fact that we are women means we've failed a litmus test for doing business with some people. Technology, gaming, comic books and graphic novels, construction, and manufacturing—just to name a few—are industries where women are held to vastly different standards, constantly having to prove themselves not just to get a job but to be respected on a day-to-day basis. Unfortunately, that's how the medical cannabis industry has started out here in Maryland for us.

"No, I'm afraid we don't have the volume at this time."

Figures.

■ ■ ■

Exclusive boys' clubs were just one of the problems with getting product in the early days. Another problem was how little cannabis there was to buy. Though cannabis had operated underground for decades, it was only now seeing the kind of serious development afforded a legal product. Cannabis was so new that no one in the industry had a firm idea of how to process, package, market, and distribute it—everyone was busy trying new things and seeing what stuck. The state tried its hardest to do its due diligence when approving licenses for growing and processing operations, but in the end, even the state had no idea how it would turn out. Theories on the regulation of business is one thing—how a business actually behaves and performs is another.

In theory, the model is pretty straightforward. Growers grow the plant, processors process the plant into a number of different products, and dispensaries (like Greenhouse Wellness) dispense the product. But there are still a lot of unknowns concerning which type of product to focus on. While some patients prefer the flower (the term used for buds of unprocessed cannabis people smoked and bought—illegally, of course—in baggies before it started to become legalized), the beginning of the legal market allowed for processors to do some meaningful experimentation with ways to consume cannabis. Today, cannabis can be

- vaped;
- cooked into food (called "edibles" by most dispensaries);
- ingested through drink or tincture;
- chewed in gum;
- infused in topicals like creams, oils, and lotions;
- infused into suppositories (for those who deal with severe nausea); and
- taken as a tablet, either chewed or swallowed.

■ ■ ■

When we finally got product in our store in December 2017 (a year after our bid was accepted), there were only two suppliers in the game: one that provided flower (the plant matter that most people are familiar with) and one that provided elixirs and tablets. So even though Leslie and I had done all that research on which types of cannabis would be the best and healthiest for our patients, we were still bound by what was available.

When we started accepting consultations, we saw that the average age of our patients was over sixty. Though we saw some older patients who smoked cigarettes, and who probably wouldn't mind smoking cannabis, we made the judgment that most of our patients wouldn't be comfortable smoking it. Leslie, as a doctor, was squarely against smoking anyway, and I tended to agree that smoking probably wasn't the best. After all, we were working hard to subvert the popular perception of cannabis, and there was a profound stigma attached to smoking. So despite the limitations in product, we sought to sell mostly concentrates from cannabis processors.

We learned pretty early on that most dispensaries had a flower-to-concentrate ratio of about 70 percent to 30 percent. We set out to reverse that: 70 percent concentrate to 30 percent flower. Others in the medical cannabis community, who were already baffled by how we'd decided to set up our dispensary, were further baffled by our choice in product. They'd say things like "You girls have it all wrong."

I swear, I'd never been called "girl" so much in my life. And this was 2017, and I am nearly sixty years old. "How could this be?" you might ask. Most folks think that the cannabis industry belongs to liberal-minded people, and they could be forgiven for thinking that: most people who support cannabis legalization are left of center. Though the cannabis debate is presented as a black-and-white, liberal versus conservative battle at the macro level of American politics, people are more complex than that: I've met plenty of conservative proponents of legal cannabis, just like I've met plenty of liberal people who aren't fully on board with gender equality. In my experience, some of the self-proclaimed male "feminists" and "allies" end up being among the most disappointing offenders. They *believe* they're all in on social equality, but their behavior suggests otherwise. We're all creatures of our biases, and even those who call themselves feminists are fighting against ages of ingrained perceptions. They're often hurtful without realizing they're being hurtful.

And so it was with a lot of men in the cannabis industry—mostly liberal-minded men who *in theory* would be open to doing business with women but somehow weren't quite there.

At this point in my career, I knew how to deal with men who belittled me. If I felt I was being denied product because I wasn't a part of the boys' club, I found a different way to get product; if a male cannabis grower thought it was OK to call me "girl," I went ahead and went with my instinct anyway.

It took a long, long time to get to that point, of course. My very first job, soon after I got my engineering degree, was for a company supporting avionic equipment for the US Navy. I was the first female engineer to be hired at this rather large company. Good on them for hiring a woman, but since I was the first, there were some initial difficulties. The debate on my first day of work was "Do we put her in the secretarial bay with the gals or in an office with a man? Well, we can't put her with a man—their wives might have a problem, or they won't be comfortable." Who knew that was an issue? I ended up in an office with another woman that they had hired as a logistician. This was 1983, so it wasn't totally *unheard* of for women to be in such a workplace, but then again, it kind of was: I was their first female engineer, after all. I didn't think much of it at first, but then came the harassment.

I was from a small town; I didn't really know what harassment was. When I heard a man say, "You look nice," I took it at face value—though I would learn that sometimes they're *really* saying, "You look sexy." Then I would start hearing things like "On our trip to California, how about you sleep in my room?"

I was married, but that didn't stop gentlemen (a very generous term) from harassing me. At that point in my career, I was more concerned with fitting in than stemming obnoxious behavior. I became a pro at defusing a situation with a joke or "What would your wife say?" I would ask the bartender to serve me water in a shot glass when the guys were having shots. There were no other female engineers to emulate, so I made my own boundaries and tried not to offend anyone along the way. But eventually it got so bad that I left for another job.

Unfortunately, some of the same behavior was waiting for me at my next job—and at the job after that. The thing about institutional biases is that they're *everywhere*. When I adopted my first child, my employer said to me, "Women in sales aren't mothers, and adoption isn't our issue. So we'll let you take two weeks of vacation." That was it. I could only take two weeks of vacation with a new child. This was a sign of the times. Fortunately, the Parental and Medical Leave Act of 1988 was a godsend to families, both men and women. By the time my second child came, employers recognized and honored adoption leave.

Despite the harassment and unfairness, I didn't complain. I didn't even tell many people about it. And to this day, I feel guilty. Guilty for not smoothing it out for the next woman. Like most women, I just felt guilty that I, in some way, *encouraged* this behavior. There's a saying I like: "Empowered women empower women." So true—but back in 1984, I was not empowered. I go back to the Maya Angelou quote: "Each time a woman stands up for herself, without knowing it possibly, without claiming it, she stands up for all women." I'm sorry, girlfriends; I failed you then. But I won't fail you now.

Fortunately, things are getting better for rank-and-file women in the workplace. Everyone is getting more used to the idea of women at work. Now if only society could get more used to women *owning* and *running* businesses. That's where I hope Leslie and I can make a difference. Gender roles are so deeply conditioned in us that we often capitulate to them, even when they chafe. One of the ways women do this is by making ourselves smaller, quieter, less bright. We are afraid of negative attention, the idea that we could bring bad things on ourselves by drawing attention, and even just that we don't want to outshine someone else because it will seem "'bossy," "bitchy," or "conceited."

Girls are taught to be "naturally beautiful" in ways that are difficult—if not impossible—to achieve naturally. They're taught to be sexy but not sexual. The idea is often that we should be exceptional in some way that will make us appealing but not so much that we stand out above the crowd—if we do, we're a target for either ridicule or hatred. Feminism and femininity are not mutually exclusive.

By the time Leslie and I got Greenhouse Wellness on its feet, I had started, run, and invested in businesses for a few decades, but I kept running into the same old scenario: men not taking me seriously and doubting that I knew what I was doing. Even the larger institutional barriers made business more difficult.

Once Leslie and I learned that our bid had been accepted, we tried to replicate the magic by submitting similar medical cannabis bids in Ohio and Pennsylvania. However, both of these bids failed spectacularly. It was very humbling after our great win in Maryland. That's one thing in business: a lot of the time, you're going to fail. Even after you succeed, you fail. All you can do is figure out why, do your homework, and figure out how to turn failure into success.

Our Maryland bid was successful in part because our names were removed from it, and we got in by virtue of our ideas. This helped even the playing field between passionate independent businesspeople like us and the giant business interests. But Ohio and Pennsylvania had no such blind bids, allowing the large business interests to make full use of their considerable advantages.

The Pennsylvania bid was particularly troubling. We were confused how our proposal for that state could have scored so low when our Maryland bid scored so high. When we appealed the decision, we discovered that part of the reason was because we'd scored so poorly in the diversity plan—an effort by the state to ensure that not just white men got hired. We were a little too diligent in this regard: we figured since we were two women, and our staff already included minorities, our diversity plan should involve hiring more men. However, the cookie-cutter nature of the review process flagged that as unacceptable, and our bid got rejected. In other words, we got penalized because the state failed to allow for the possibility of a business that *wasn't* owned and operated by white men. One of the great goals of my life has been to upend that way of thinking. I clearly have a long way to go.

The state's well-meaning but flawed effort to foster diversity doomed us in Pennsylvania. It was that and having to compete with large corporations—including the massive publicly traded ones from Canada, where cannabis had been legalized federally. And that's not all: the blind bid gave a small dispensary like us a modest leg up in Maryland, but the corporations certainly aren't waiting on the sidelines.

While Maryland law says that you can own one dispensary, many of the large companies have five under their management. They're circumventing the rules by putting the dispensaries under a management agreement, which means they get 99 percent of the profits. It's an elegant solution and a loophole that can't be closed for now, and it's a problem for a small company like Greenhouse Wellness.

■ ■ ■

Allow me to take a step back for a moment. As an experienced, pragmatic businesswoman, I understand why large corporations exist. Those who found and operate conglomerates spend years (or decades) building effective infrastructure that elevates whole industries. They have the institutional knowledge and the resources necessary to create thousands of jobs and efficiently deliver goods and services to the maximum number of people. But when they get too big, it's a recipe for exploitation and innovative stagnation. Competition—the cornerstone of capitalism—becomes a joke.

I can draw a clear line from giant corporations to the cannabis boys' clubs shutting us out of lucrative deals. In fact, I might say that most corporations simply *are* giant boys' clubs. After all, the vast majority of chief executives are men, and the workforce at large is still disproportionately male. But I take solace in the fact that the marketplace *is* realizing that small businesses have a valuable perspective—and so do women.

In many ways, business is a vast classroom. But one way it *isn't* like a classroom is that no one is going to call on us ladies to provide our views or hand us opportunities to show off our talents. We have to *speak up*. We have to *demand* attention. And when we speak up, we have to be prepared to be shut down, ignored, or even harassed. And when that happens, we must have the courage to stand by our instincts. We need to ask the difficult questions, like "Why are we being denied a deal on a certain volume of cannabis?"

Leslie and I have been lucky enough (and perhaps savvy or determined enough) to find success in this business despite efforts to exclude us or belittle our way of doing things. Still, I don't want to pretend that we have all the answers. Though we have plenty of fresh new ideas about medical cannabis, we've also learned to give the proper respect to what's come before us: the tried-and-true methods that allowed the industry to come this far.

For example, we decided that smoking is bad and scoffed at the idea of providing so much flower to our patients. But Leslie and I would later come around to it. As effective as concentrates are, nature is the best engineer—the plant itself offers benefits that aren't necessarily present in concentrates. And as far as smoking goes, cannabis is a healthier option than cigarettes. We still heavily favor concentrates; we never recommend smoking flower as a first option, and we often recommend vaping the flower instead. Bottom line, we respect the role of the cannabis flower in the industry and in healing, and we remain open minded to what will come next. We have our own body of knowledge, but we also listen to what our patients tell us they want and need.

And that right there is the big difference between a small cannabis business like Greenhouse Wellness and a cannabis conglomerate. Our focus, by necessity, is on our patients. Though a large corporation might claim to have the patient's best interests at heart, it's only insofar as that patient can boost profits. The bigger a company gets, the further removed the decision makers are from people they purport to serve. I mean this literally: it's easy to forget a patient's needs when you're on the sixtieth floor of a skyscraper. Out of sight, out of mind.

Leslie and I, on the other hand, look our patients in the eyes. They aren't data points on a vast spreadsheet; they're real people who need real care. We have a business to run, of course, but we can't let profits outshine our obligation to our patients and our community.

CHAPTER 7

The most beautiful people we have known
are those who have known defeat, known
suffering, known struggle, known loss, and
have found their way out of the depths. These
persons have an appreciation, a sensitivity and
an understanding of life that fills them with
compassion, gentleness, and a deep loving
concern. Beautiful people do not just happen.
—Elizabeth Kubler-Ross

Leslie

"Just give me whatever has the highest THC," he said, tapping his fingers on the quartz countertop, his eyes darting to the large monitor that listed cannabis products.

Judging by this man's request and his appearance—unshaven, a little too long without a haircut, and baggy clothes—I had pegged him as what we in the business call "a stoner." Gina and I had worked hard to position Greenhouse Wellness as a medically focused dispensary that genuinely cared about providing medicine to people who needed it. But we weren't ignorant to the possibility of people just looking to get a legal high under Uncle Sam's nose. I'd been trained not to judge someone by their appearance, but this guy was making it difficult.

"OK, here are a few of our options," I said. "Can I ask what condition you're looking to treat?" This was the second time I'd asked this question, though in a slightly different way. As a physician, I'd been trained to ask patients questions three times to give them three opportunities to tell the truth about what was *really* happening.

"I'm really just looking for whatever has the highest THC." I kept a straight face and nodded, careful not to betray any sense of impatience or frustration. It *was* frustrating, though. Whenever someone came in asking for the product with the highest THC (also known as the psychoactive component of cannabis), it was like someone going to a wine store and asking for a bottle of Everclear. They were clearly not looking for something they'd enjoy or that would help them: they wanted something that would mess them up.

After going on for a couple minutes about the different kinds of strains and their effects, I said, "But this all depends on what kind of ailment you need help with." The third time must have really been the charm, because something changed in this gentleman. He threw up his hands—but then he took in a deep breath, and his demeanor softened. Tears formed in his eyes as he told me about his experience in the military and how he was suffering with profound anxiety. Once we spoke openly about his PTSD, I felt like I could actually help him. His shoulders relaxed as if a tremendous weight had lifted off him. I directed him toward the products I believed would ease his suffering, and they certainly weren't the strains with the highest THC.

When he came in, I made an assumption about this man based on his appearance, but once I got him to be honest with me, I made what I believed was serious progress toward his healing. A medical cannabis dispensary that didn't place such an emphasis on medicine might have immediately satisfied this man's initial request and sent him on his way. And that wouldn't have provided him the type of help he needed.

■ ■ ■

That's the key difference between what we do and what others do. Our patrons aren't customers—they're *patients*. It's important to note that this gentleman didn't just come in from the street. Like other medical cannabis users, he submitted an online patient application from the MMCC, obtained a written certification from a physician registered with the MMCC, and received a state-issued patient ID card. He followed state protocol to get into the building, and we followed ours to make sure he got the right treatment.

Our consultation process lies at the center of our care strategy. Once a patient comes in for a consultation, we work to make them as comfortable as possible. After welcoming them to Greenhouse Wellness, we will invite them into a private but spacious consultation room and ask a series of questions: "What brings you here? Is this your first time? What ailment are you trying to treat? What treatments have you tried? What are you taking right now? What diseases have you had in the past? When did your symptoms start? What is your pain level? What kind of stress do you feel? Are you sleeping enough? Could more sleep help solve some of your other problems?"

And then we ask, "What is your previous experience with cannabis?" Sometimes the answer is "I tried it once in college" or

"I smoke occasionally." Other times it's "I smoke every day," or more commonly "I've never tried cannabis." Sometimes they hesitate, sometimes they blush, but we make it as clear as possible that there is absolutely no judgment, and we encourage them to tell the truth.

I believe that before a medical professional can provide effective treatment to a patient, the patient must be completely honest about what they're going through. Still, some patients are so intimidated by the setting, the pressures from their insurance providers, and the white coats that they feel it's necessary to lie or withhold the truth. But we work hard to create an atmosphere that's as comfortable and welcoming as possible. We do every bit as much due diligence as the medical staff at a general practitioner's office, but we don't wear white coats, and we don't put a laptop between ourselves and our patients. At the end of a visit, I'll give a patient a high five and congratulate them on having the courage to come visit us, because I know it's not easy.

One of the things that frustrated me about my training as a doctor—stemming back to my time in med school—was the formal, stilted way we were trained to interact with our patients, addressing them as "Mr. So-and-So." While a part of me understood the reasons for maintaining emotional distance with patients, this always seemed to me like a holdover from the Victorian era, when decorum reigned supreme. I always preferred to get down and dirty with my patients and establish a rapport as quickly as possible. I found that to be a more effective means of discovering what was *really* going on, and I was happy to bring that philosophy to Greenhouse Wellness. It worked for the "stoner" who came in looking for a high-THC product, and it's worked for hundreds of other patients. And in turn, the cannabis worked to alleviate their symptoms.

■ ■ ■

Let me be absolutely clear what *worked* means. I don't believe that cannabis can cure everything, and I always make sure my patients have reasonable expectations. While I've seen cannabis reduce stress, ease pain, improve appetites, and help patients get to sleep, it cannot cure terminal illnesses by itself. Still, we've seen cannabis give terminally ill patients more time with their loved ones and vastly improve quality of life.

I recall one patient who came to us with his wife. He was confined to a wheelchair, his whole body listed to the side, and he looked exhausted, like he had waged a long battle and was nearing the end of his ability to fight. He wore Superman pajama pants because they were comfortable—but the more I learned about him, the more I would come to think of them as a symbol of his courage and inner strength.

This man was near Ground Zero during the 9/11 attack, and the toxic dust was catastrophic to his health. He was only in his late forties, but he had been diagnosed with renal cell carcinoma that had spread to his spine. He'd lost bowel and bladder function and function in his legs, and he was in horrific pain.

After analyzing his illness, symptoms, current medications, and medical history, we started him on a cannabis protocol that his wife would go to great lengths to prepare for him. Before long, he started regaining function. He regained some feeling in his legs, he got his catheter taken out, he became continent again—he even started driving again with the help of hand controls. He was hungry for food, he was more active, and he was more able to participate in his young kids' lives. Most importantly, his pain was controlled without the use of debilitating opioids, and his quality of life was therefore substantially improved.

Unfortunately, he eventually passed away from cancer, as many of our patients do, but before he did, he had the physical ability and presence of mind to dictate heartfelt letters to his children for the major events to come in their lives: birthdays, graduations, weddings, and, eventually, the births of their own kids. These will be invaluable messages to his beloved children, making it possible for him to keep being their Superman even though he won't be around for them physically.

Gina and I were deeply honored to be involved in his final months and to help him give his family one last gift. But most of all we were blown away by his courage and the incredible support from his wife. We know that the caregivers carry so much weight. The combination of dealing with a sick loved one and the stigma of turning to medical cannabis is so very difficult. This gentleman's wife helped him and stayed strong for his family and their children. Her courage was and is amazing, and it has left a lasting mark on Gina and me.

Caregivers are an essential part of working with the terminally ill. Their work is filled with dedication; it is amazing and profound in its worth. We have seen caregivers go to almost any lengths for their loved ones. They inspire us with their kindness, generosity, and selflessness.

We get heavily involved in the lives of our patients. We have a box of tissues in every room of the dispensary because there's a lot of crying—sometimes it's our patients, sometimes us, sometimes both. We feel their heartbreak and joy, and we work hard to make sure they have medicine that will improve their quality of life for as long as possible. And after all that we've seen, we know that cannabis can be helpful medicine.

■ ■ ■

I get it. I see why some people refuse to believe cannabis is anything but a dangerous drug. Staunch defenders of cannabis always talk about how no one has ever died from an overdose of cannabis, but many have died while under its influence. Like any substance, it's dangerous when used to excess, and I won't pretend it's a 100 percent safe miracle plant.

What upsets me the most about the cannabis industry are the growers who breed only cannabis with the highest possible concentration of THC. It feels a little bit like they're doing this just because they can—not because they're trying to help anyone. Instead, they're trying to get people higher, and they aren't doing the cannabis industry any favors. Though to be fair, they're responding to the demands of the market, which is sadly not medically based and not all that based in solid science. But unless the growers change their practice, we can't begin to unwind a big part of what's wrong with the industry currently. The further cannabis gets from its natural roots, the further it gets from its natural benefits. The higher the THC, the closer cannabis gets to earning its Schedule I designation (along with heroin and cocaine). I understand others' concern with this, because it's also my concern. But that's not the kind of cannabis I seek to give people as medicine.

Cannabis and humans have been linked since before recorded time. You might say we evolved together. And there have been plenty of mentions of medical cannabis throughout the ages, spanning back to its first known recorded use in China around 2000 BCE. Throughout most of human history, it was considered safe and beneficial and—for thousands of years after we developed laws—legal. It was only after a bizarre propaganda campaign (buoyed by profound misunderstanding) that it actually became illegal in the United States in 1937. That propaganda sustained the prohibition of cannabis for decades, up through the Nancy Reagan "Just Say No" era and beyond. It's only now that we're beginning to understand how exactly cannabis can help us, but there are so many roadblocks to getting people this affordable, plentiful, and beneficial medicine.

As a physician classically trained in Western medicine, I've been taught to only accept evidence-based information accumulated through randomized, controlled trials. Western doctors like me critically analyze studies to see if they're worthwhile, identify flaws, and extrapolate data that can be used to help patients. The only trouble is that there are no robust, randomized, controlled trials for federally illegal substances—including cannabis. It's a catch-22: there are no studies because it's illegal, and it's illegal because there haven't been enough studies to show the skeptics that it's worth considering. As a physician who recommends cannabis, all I can do is analyze what modest studies *are* out there and do my best to match patients with appropriate treatment.

Despite the lack of studies—or at least the kind of studies afforded a drug eligible for FDA approval—public opinion has shifted enough for cannabis to be legalized in some capacity in thirty-three states as of this writing. In a way, you might consider this slow rollout to be its own type of experimentation, though not exactly randomized and certainly not controlled.

Every day, more people shift their opinion on cannabis a little more toward acceptance, and more people try it to see what the fuss is about. The more people who try it, the more they feel relief from their symptoms or just feel *better* (especially when directed by a medical professional). In medicine, they tell you not to give weight to anecdotal evidence when making conclusions. But how many anecdotes do you need until you have data? We've seen cannabis help so many of our patients that it's hard not to be a believer in its positive effects.

■ ■ ■

While Gina and I are pleased to see cannabis's trajectory bend toward legalization, and we know that further acceptance will ultimately further increase the drug's potential for wellness, we're also frustrated. We're frustrated knowing that there are millions of people out there suffering from a litany of terrible ailments but who don't have reliable access to legal cannabis, which can make a profound difference in the quality of their lives, if not help *save* their lives.

Even in Maryland, which legalized medical cannabis in 2013, the slow bureaucratic rollout rendered us unable to provide medicine to patients who needed it late in 2017. I recall one man whose wife was suffering from glioblastoma multiforme, a terrible form of brain cancer. The little cannabis evidence we'd seen suggested that cannabis could have a marked effect on relieving some of the symptoms of this particular tumor, including seizures. We could have helped her—eased her suffering or even given her more quality time with her family—but her disease was too advanced by the time we finally got product to sell, and she passed away soon after we opened. Our frustration and helplessness with being unable to help this couple paled in comparison to the heartbreak they must have felt in dealing with the disease—with having potentially helpful medicine so close to their grasp, yet unattainable.

If nothing else, we would wish cannabis to be legal for the terminally ill. At that point in a person's illness, we believe all the controversy surrounding the drug falls away. Many who suffer from a terminal illness have had their hope and strength sapped by radiation, chemotherapy, surgery, and trial drugs—what more could they have to lose by trying cannabis? And maybe they even have something to gain. When you're up against the wall, we believe in using every potentially beneficial drug in the arsenal, and we think that sparing patients from the taxing side effects of more "traditional" treatments could have a marked effect on quality of life when employed earlier in the illness's course.

It's all frustrating, but most of all, we're exasperated that such a relatively benign drug could be illegal while sledgehammer drugs like opioids remain legal. I understand the role opioids play in medicine, and I believe they can be helpful in certain situations, but there is no doubt that they are being abused in this country. Every day, 130 people die from opioid overdose while pharmaceutical company profits soar—profits that, by the way, go to politicians, who nurture an interest to keep things exactly the way they are.

Big Pharma, for all the good it does in a number of areas, is broken in a lot of ways. For one, it operates under the auspices of Western medicine. Again, there is a lot about Western medicine I support and agree with—I believe in science, and I know we owe so much of our modern prosperity to evidence-based medicine—but from what I've seen, Big Pharma and Western medicine are so focused on short-term solutions that they lose sight of the bigger picture. Antibiotics for an infection instead of figuring out how to prevent the infection. Steroids for inflammation instead of determining how to prevent the inflammation. Opioids for the pain instead of stopping the pain at the source. This paradigm makes sense, when you think about it—if someone is cured of a condition, they have no more need of the medication, and the pharmaceutical company loses a customer. You might say that Big Pharma is addicted to these short-term solutions—every bit as addicted as millions of people are to their products.

Cannabis doesn't have the capabilities of some pharmaceuticals. I would never tell someone just diagnosed with breast cancer to initiate a 100 percent cannabis regimen. But what cannabis *does* do is support your body's natural ability to heal itself. Any doctor will tell you that medicine doesn't heal the body directly— rather, it helps the body heal itself. And the body does its job most effectively when it's operating at optimum capacity. The reason I believe cannabis is so beneficial is because it clears the way for the body and other medicines to do their work. Is your insomnia prolonging your sickness? Try some cannabis to help you get to sleep. Is stress increasing your risk of heart disease? Let cannabis bring down your heart rate. Is your lack of appetite depriving you of essential nutrients? Well, have you ever heard of the munchies?

The full benefits of cannabis are unknown. But we already know enough to confidently say that its benefits are substantial. Even recreational cannabis, which perhaps makes skeptics the most nervous, has its own potential to benefit users. After all, I believe that many recreational users are treating something, whether they're conscious of it or not. Some might use cannabis when they're depressed, or others might use it to take the edge off (i.e., reduce their anxiety). That gentleman who I pegged as a "stoner" was hoping to self-medicate his PTSD with high-THC cannabis. As far as self-medicating goes, cannabis beats alcohol, and it sure as hell beats opioids. Just imagine how much good cannabis can do once more people begin learning about the subtle differences in cannabis strains and products—once the national conversation moves from back-alley whispers to unabashed public discourse, and the considerable brainpower behind medical science finally gets a chance to study cannabis openly and thoroughly.

■ ■ ■

One of our patients, Dawn, who is living with multiple sclerosis, has offered testimony of her experience with traditional drugs and cannabis:

> Living with multiple sclerosis has affected me in many ways. Number one, my ability to walk. Also, cognitive issues—sometimes you get a little bit of a brain fog with MS because of where the lesions are located on your brain. Previously I have been using prescribed medication from my neurologist. There were many side effects and things that I wasn't expecting. I wasn't feeling so well, and it would make me cry on the weekends because the only options at that time for MS were three drugs: the ABC drugs. The first drug was an injection—a long needle. I had to inject myself. It would make me exhausted beyond explanation. You just have to feel it. I don't want anybody to feel that type of exhaustion. I experienced flu-like symptoms every single time I injected myself. The worst flu you've ever had.
>
> I said, "You know what? I'm not going to do this to myself for months and months and months for the rest of my life; there's no way." Because there is no cure for MS. For about nine years, I was a noncompliant patient, and I went off of all drugs. I said, "Forget this—I'm doing everything holistic." At the time, medical cannabis was not approved anywhere; I desperately wanted to try, and I kept saying, "As soon as they approve it, I want to try this."
>
> My perception of cannabis was you're always high. You're just sitting back, and you're just kind of in a catatonic, mellow mood the whole time you're smoking. And I found that isn't the case. I feel as if I can get up in the

morning, I can make breakfast, I can make lunch, I can actually plan out the entire day and then have time for myself—have time for my son. And so now I'm just using the cannabis with my positive attitude, and my overall well-being is so much better. I feel good when I wake up. I have energy. I feel like there is hope. I can get my life back, and I'm still a young person, so I still want to enjoy life as much as I can.

Not long ago we saw Dawn walk into our dispensary without her cane—the first time we'd seen her without it. Another patient has used cannabis to get off painkillers and liberate himself from crippling side effects. Yet another was able to return to the workforce after a long absence caused by cervical dystonia. We've already seen hundreds of patients improve their lives with cannabis, and we see more every day. We hope perceptions of cannabis change—and laws with them—but in the meantime, we're content to keep our heads down and keep doing good work for our patients.

CHAPTER 8

We need to reshape our own perception
of how we view ourselves. We have to
step up as women and take the lead.
— BEYONCÉ

Gina

On the outside, I was trying my hardest to maintain my bright West Virginia smile—but inside I was absolutely terrified. Our humble dispensary was overrun by patients, with dozens more waiting outside, and we were completely unprepared. We didn't have enough registers or enough staff members working, and folks were growing increasingly impatient with the long wait. I made desperate eye contact with Leslie. She would later tell me, "You looked like how I felt."

It was April 20, 2018—or as we say in the cannabis business, "4/20." Though Leslie and I were well aware of the significance of 4/20 in cannabis culture, we didn't quite grasp that April 20 was such a major holiday. We expected it was mostly for the recreational users and that our patients and prospective patients—who were mostly keen on the medicinal properties of cannabis—wouldn't be interested. In the morning huddle, I'd told the staff, "It might be a little busier today, but it should be more or less normal." Little did I know that about thirty people had already lined up at the door. Just goes to show how much, or how little, I knew about the industry.

Our first patient that day was an eighty-four-year-old woman in mom jeans and a cat T-shirt using a walker with tennis balls. She'd heard the hoopla about 4/20 and wanted to be a part of it, so here she was, having the time of her life. The patients that followed came from every walk of life, and they had varying degrees of enthusiasm and patience. All told, we must have seen around three hundred people—way up from the fifty or so we might have seen on a normal Friday.

A normal day would have been much less chaotic. Despite the lack of preparation for 4/20, Greenhouse Wellness was a well-oiled machine. After our morning huddle, we'd roll out a series of carts and restock sold-out products (Maryland law requires all products to be locked up at night, hence the movable carts). Then we'd review the day's specials and training info for the team and go about the business of serving our patients.

When patients first enter the building, they come to a waiting room, where a receptionist checks to see that they're certified and have an active doctor certification. The patient then gets called into the dispensary proper, where they can browse products and speak with our wellness consultants. Patients can also call ahead to schedule a private thirty-minute consultation with Leslie on Mondays or with our eminently qualified wellness consultants on other days of the week. Patients who already know what they want can be in and out in three minutes, while those who want to browse and talk might be there for the better part of an hour.

Of course, in order to get patients in the door, they need to know about us. We stay active on Facebook and Instagram, and we keep existing patients in the loop with text and email updates on the latest news and specials. Keeping up on both Facebook and Instagram requires caution, as dispensaries' social media pages can be taken down if these platforms receive notices that they are connected with cannabis. Yes, you can have a group, but if you talk about pricing or selling, down you go, and all your followers with you. Every week we do a "Medical Monday" YouTube video, where we discuss a variety of topics, including cannabis delivery systems, the various properties of different cannabis strains, and how cannabis can help treat specific ailments. Our outreach efforts, our bedside manner, our skilled staff, and our unique approach to medical cannabis all contribute to an effective formula that works for our patients and lends itself to success.

■ ■ ■

Let me back up and say that starting and running a business (any business) is a daunting endeavor—I know this as well as anyone. Many people fail at it. Many go bankrupt. If you're a young woman at the beginning of your career, you might look at Greenhouse Wellness and think, *I couldn't put all that together*. Let me tell you that even if that's true now, you won't think that way forever. You can do it. You will make mistakes and might need a do-over, but if you want it, you will do it.

Leslie and I didn't just luck into this formula, and Greenhouse Wellness wasn't my first business. Though cannabis was totally new to me, I'd already accumulated a career's worth of business knowledge and instincts. I'd made lots of mistakes and learned a ton, and *then* I funneled my years of experience into a successful medical cannabis dispensary.

Every path is different, and most require a lot of hard work—mine certainly did. After years of working as an engineer, I switched gears and went into sales. The transition was gradual. At first I was the translator between engineering and sales, which was shocking to an introvert like myself. But I loved sales; it was a chessboard that required strategy and thought. After adopting my second child, I decided I would scale back, and I eventually became the first salesperson in the computer security company Trusted Information Systems.

They had a great product and just needed "translation" between engineering and sales. I was surrounded by the smartest people I had *ever* met. I swear they could do differential calculus in their heads, but they couldn't sell. It just wasn't their nature or calling. It was a wonderful experience to grow a sales team, do the initial public offering road show, and take the company public. After the company sold to McAfee, I was fortunate to start a venture fund with the founder of Trusted Information Systems, Stephen Walker. He is one of the nicest and kindest men I have ever had the good fortune to meet, and I absolutely loved the venture fund. We saw thousands of plans in a year and worked hard to invest in the best and brightest.

Working hard got me far, and working *smart* got me further. But even then I didn't have enough faith in myself to start my own business. It wasn't until after we'd funded about fifty budding businesses—and the right idea came along—that I decided it was time to go into business for myself.

OK, I'll be honest: sometimes luck *does* have something to do with success, but it's never luck alone. One day I went to the doctor to have her close a vein in my face with a laser. The procedure took about twenty seconds, and then the doctor said, "Here's a bag of frozen peas for the soreness."

I said, "My God, isn't there anything else?"

She said, "No, not right now." But then she started talking about an idea she had: a small, handy package that could go hot or cold for twenty minutes. Deep down, I was still an engineer, so I went home, looked up the thermal conductivity required, and wrote a little spider to comb through the internet for specific information (a spider is a small program that "crawls" websites and looks for phrases or words and then reports back its findings—kind of like a proto-Google). A couple of months later, the spider returned with the information that a company in China had this polymer gel bead that could keep hot or cold for twenty minutes. So I called the doctor up and said, "Is this what you're talking about?"

It was. And before long, we decided to start a business selling thermal gel packs that could be hot or cold for twenty minutes. That was the genesis of TheraPearl, a company that would blossom into a global enterprise and put me on a *Forbes* "Women Who Built Outstanding Companies" list. Yes, it was luck that put me in a room with a doctor who had this brilliant idea, but it was decades of experience (and luck, hard work, and good fortune) that enabled me to act on that idea and turn it into something. How does that saying go? Something like "When God closes a vein, she opens a window"?

Two additional partners with amazing retail expertise were the special sauce to get into the commercial space. The TheraPearl team was amazing. We hired young, earnest, hardworking kids—often straight out of school. I can truly say that they taught me so much. They didn't know that they couldn't do something—so they did it! We also had a young man with a disability, Ryan, who worked for us. Ryan taught us kindness. It still brings tears to my eyes when I remember the young professionals tying his shoes and trying to explain things to Ryan. He made us all better.

After we sold TheraPearl to BioFreeze, I was no longer frightened by the prospect of starting my own business. I had the will, the experience, and the means necessary to embark on another venture. And when Leslie and I came across the opportunity to get into medical cannabis, everything fell into place—though again, there was plenty of work involved.

■ ■ ■

My path to success is unique to me, but it isn't particularly unusual for any woman to imagine. No matter who you are, you can use your experience and skills—plus a little bit of patience and luck and *a lot* of hard work—to climb toward your goals…or perhaps toward some unknown endeavor you didn't realize you were climbing to. After all, I never thought I'd be involved in cannabis.

Still, *easy* isn't the word I'd use to describe it. And as difficult as it is for men, it's even more difficult for women. How do I know this? Let me put it this way: Could you ever in a thousand years imagine *Forbes* publishing a list titled "Men Who Built Outstanding Companies"? Virtually *every* business, outstanding or otherwise, is built by a man. The mere fact that they would make such a list for women is proof that it's somehow novel and newsworthy for women to start their own businesses. That means too many of us are on the sidelines. Part of it is because it's a little harder for us to reach a man's level of success. Part of it is because we *think* it's hard, so we don't even try. I always laugh and say, "When *woman* stops being an adjective to describe someone, then equality will reign."

I get it. It was plenty hard for me. As a young female engineer and the first female engineer in the company, where I would sit became an issue. I couldn't work in the same office as the male engineers because I might make their wives uncomfortable. I really wasn't a secretary, but perhaps the secretarial bay was a better option. In the end, I was put into an office with another talented female. While that "solution" made sense to my male colleagues, it was like a pair of concrete stilettos in terms of my own career. Lord only knows how many productive conversations I was excluded from. How many happy hours, golf games, and trips to the strip club I wasn't invited to. How many relationships and networking opportunities I was denied—all because I was an engineer with the wrong parts.

Thinking about this makes me both angry and disappointed. But then I think about what *they* missed out on. By exiling me to the women's office, they missed out on my voice, my vision, my drive. Unfulfilled and underutilized, I left that job, and then I left engineering altogether. Sometimes I think about what I *could* have contributed to that company and to engineering if I'd been treated as an equal. I left after being harassed by my manager. At the time, I blamed myself and the situation and just left quietly. I still feel guilty about it for the women after me, and I won't do that again. But I don't think about it for too long. After all, I found a path I like just fine.

And yet the path I ended up on was *still* littered with obstacles. There were small ones, like being interrupted countless times by booming male voices, and then there were big ones, like being denied adequate time off for maternity leave: when I worked in sales, my supervisor only gave me two weeks off to care for my newly adopted daughter. I ended up leaving that job too.

But as a female professional, you can't just follow the path of least resistance. If you're denied opportunities in one field, it's not so easy to pick up your skirts and move to another. I did it a couple of times: for reasons beyond "It got tough," sure, but I'd be lying if I said that wasn't a factor. Fortunately for me, exploring so many different fields (what I like to call "repotting" myself) would give me the breadth of experience I needed to reach higher than I might have if I'd stuck to any one field.

I would come to realize that for a woman to succeed—for *women* to succeed—we eventually need to stare down the biggest, scariest impediments to our success and shatter them. If you shatter enough impediments, you get to be the boss, and that's when things can *really* change.

When we started TheraPearl, we did things our way. We fostered a culture of kindness, cooperation, and equality. My partners, Gary Rezeppa and Daniel Baumwald, were key to that happening. When our marketing director had her child, we offered her several months off with pay (we didn't have a pregnancy program) because we saw the long-term value of helping an employee establish a happy and healthy family home—so then she could return to work knowing her child had a good start in life.

■ ■ ■

When Leslie and I started Greenhouse Wellness, we ran into plenty more impediments: some unique to us as women, and some that were just part of conducting business—federally illegal business, I might add. We've stood firm against and shattered many of those impediments already, and we're always looking ahead to what we should shatter next.

I understand that conflict is frightening—especially to a young businesswoman who hasn't had a full taste of it yet—but it's necessary if we're going to put an end to lists like "Women Who Built Outstanding Companies." Standing up for yourself can be terrifying, but the good news is you're not alone. You don't need to yell or scream (and play right into the unfair "emotional female" stereotype), but you do need to stand resolute and firm in your conviction. That is not the easiest of places. Self-doubt is part of every day. But being determined to be fair and kind makes it easier.

I've had the good fortune of having a brilliant, tough, compassionate friend and partner in Leslie. I've worked jobs where other women in the office undermined each other in order to gain favor with male supervisors—but we're in charge now, and though we have our rare differences of opinion, our efforts generally dovetail upward. At Greenhouse Wellness, we don't encourage our female staff members to compete with each other. We don't encourage our male staff members to compete either. Instead, we foster a partnership that allows everyone to succeed. And yes, our male staff members are an integral and necessary part of the team. We need everyone as a part of the solution.

We don't have competition; we have *coopetition*—a combination of *cooperation* and *competition* built on the premise that your gain isn't my loss, and your loss isn't my gain. Instead, there are ways for all of us to gain—even if our interests may sometimes appear at odds. A rising tide lifts all boats.

We embody the spirit of coopetition by offering our staff members business classes. We have our CFO come in for talks on how to start your own business, how to set up a website, and so on. We know that the lessons our employees learn at these talks could very well take them away from us; they might even become direct competitors. But Leslie and I like to play the long game. While we love the work our staff members do now, and we'd love for them to stay as long as they want, we recognize that they have ambitions beyond Greenhouse Wellness. We figure that the best thing we can do is help them realize those ambitions with the hope that they'll remember us fondly when they go off to do whatever they're destined to do. And if their goals line up with ours, so much the better.

■ ■ ■

As wonderful as that all sounds, Leslie and I know there are many who don't share our views. Even in the medical cannabis business, which you might expect to be relatively chill, there are plenty of folks with a more ruthless approach. Like in any other business, there are those who lean into their advantages and exploit their competitors' weaknesses, and hey, I get it. Remember, I've been around for a while; I know that big moves often involve stepping on a few toes. Yes, I have taken the knife and turned it, but I'd like to see a new approach: one that fosters healthy competition without feeling like you need to crush your competitors. Cannabis needs this approach more than most industries, as we're much more vulnerable, and too many internal struggles could bring it all down. I hope others in the business learn to see that we're stronger when we work together.

But it's hard when there are still folks who game the system to their own advantage. Let me give you an example. Maryland granted about a hundred licenses to dispensaries on the condition that they open within a year. Greenhouse Wellness was one of the thirty or so dispensaries that complied with this rule—even though we had to operate for a few months without product, which ended up costing us dearly. Two years later, they're still allowing some of the remaining seventy dispensaries to open anyway, and it's hard not to see that as a penalty for those of us who complied at great cost. As women, we're used to playing on a slanted playing field, but we *shouldn't have to be.*

We initially bid for five dispensaries, and our bid scored high enough that we *could* have gotten five, but the rules at the time only allowed an independent business like ours to open one. The corporate growers, on the other hand, came into our state and found a way to open four dispensaries via a loophole involving management agreements. And then growers had the audacity to lobby for a half dozen dispensaries in the most recent legislative session. When I came out against it, one of the growers called me up and said, "I'm disappointed in you."

There was just something off about the way he said it—like I was a thirteen-year-old with a hickey and not a nearly sixty-year-old woman who happened to be his professional equal. His tone and his attitude struck me as a double punch of antagonism and patronization. I said, "I'm sorry you feel that way," and shared my disappointment before hanging up. Sometimes you have to smile and bite your tongue until it bleeds.

As easy as it is to burn bridges, and as good as it might have felt to say something about the horse he rode in on, that's just not the way I like to do business. The growers that also operate dispensaries may be our competitors, but they also provide the product we need for our patients. As hard as it was sometimes to stick with the coopetition ethos, I was determined to do it. Somewhere down the road, that grower may realize he needs something from me—maybe suggestions on how to run a truly medically focused dispensary—and for the betterment of the whole industry, I would provide it.

If I were to exact any kind of revenge, it would be to ensure that Greenhouse Wellness is as successful as possible. That we help as many people as possible. That our staff grows professionally and personally. All this to show that our way of doing things yields the most benefits for the most people. To show that we can learn from our mistakes and turn them into unmitigated triumphs.

■ ■ ■

Speaking of mistakes and triumphs, we learned from our ill-fated experience on April 20, 2018, and we made sure we were prepared in 2019. We had the entire staff working and extra registers to cash more people out. To keep folks from lining up at the door, we opened an hour earlier without telling anyone. We decked out the parking lot with balloons, food, games, and free coffee, and we enlisted local vendors to feed and entertain our patients as they waited for their turn. When we finally called patients in to look at product, they'd be munching their cheesesteaks, just happy as can be.

We assumed that 4/20 couldn't be any bigger than it was the previous year—especially since many more dispensaries had opened up. We were wrong. We easily saw five hundred patients. This time when Leslie and I stole glances at each other, there wasn't any panic on our faces—just pure excitement at how well everything was going.

Well, maybe a little panic. Some things, like our ability to worry, just don't change.

CHAPTER 9

She was not fragile like a flower;
She was fragile like a bomb.
— RAHUL SINGH

Leslie

I thought the attacks on my character would stop when I left my OB-GYN clinic. But the vitriol continued well after I turned my focus to my med spa and even after Gina and I started Greenhouse Wellness. If anything, the attacks increased in intensity as time went on. I've been specifically targeted, for years now, in a relentless onslaught of letters and articles fraught with false statements and sexist remarks. I've had to fight this as well as live my life and run my businesses.

But I *shouldn't have to* fight this. It shouldn't be happening at all. I've done nothing wrong—I've only stood up for what I believe in, and what I've gotten in return is a series of attacks on me and my livelihood. And what upsets me the most is how common this is for women who do anything in the public sphere.

Yes, anyone who raises their head above the vast plain of general anonymity runs the risk of public ridicule. If you do something, and people can see you doing it, there's always going to be someone to criticize you. But women have it worse. No matter how enlightened our culture gets (or *seems* to get) on gender equality, there will always be people stuck with nineteenth-century views on women. And social media, as wonderful as it is in a lot of ways, allows people to express their toxicity with little to no consequences. Some of these people are trolls who just like to see the world burn, and some are truly bitter and deranged individuals, though it's not easy to see the distinction (if there is one).

Despite my experiences, I've largely been spared the vitriol spewed by strangers online—but I see a lot of it aimed toward my female colleagues. Kait LeDonne, a marketing professional we contract to oversee our marketing efforts for Greenhouse Wellness and Blissiva, sees at least one off-color comment for every video she posts. These are videos promoting her *professional brand*, mind you, and yet men feel entitled to comment on her looks, or worse, make crude sexual statements. Recently a pair of commenters made an ungentlemanly request and questioned whether she was actually the one running her own business and left the comment "showusyourtits.com."

When that happens, anyone's instinct might be to return fire. But Kait simply screen-captured the comments and reposted them to her page with a measured, thoughtful condemnation of that behavior. When forced to confront his own comments, one of the men claimed to have been hacked. I didn't believe it then, and I don't believe it now.

There's an article from the *Washington Post* that explains a phenomenon called *crasslighting*. It's when men make crude comments online and then claim it somehow wasn't their fault: "I've been hacked," or "That wasn't meant for you," or even "Stupid autocorrect!" It's another ridiculous way men try to avoid taking responsibility for their behavior. It's worse when they say, "Can't you take a joke?" or "You're too sensitive," as if the problem is with *you* and not their crude behavior. Um, excuse me, you cannot tell me how I'm supposed to feel about your comment.

Yes, yes, I know there are many men out there who would never dream of doing such things. #NotAllMen may be technically true, but there are #EnoughMen for it to be a problem—#TooManyMen in my opinion. These men were raised in a "locker-room talk" culture that actively celebrates crude behavior. Meanwhile, women get accused of being joyless harpies when they try to speak up. I'm sick of it.

Kait and I have spoken about this at length, and she brought up a great point: the men who harass her through social media are never doing *more* than her. They're never more successful than she is. More often than not, men who hurl these comments are sad sacks who are disappointed in their own lives and jealous of Kait's. These men grew up with such privilege and entitlement that it just kills them to see a woman put herself out there and succeed more than they have.

As angry as this all makes me, and as much as I want to get down into the mud and duke it out with anyone who makes a sexist comment, a part of me knows that the best thing I can do is to be impeccably and authentically myself—to continue my streak of success and keep standing by what I believe in. Even though doing more can sometimes bring unwanted attention and negativity, I am committed to my path because at the end of the day, karma wins.

So instead of cowing to personal attacks, instead of adjusting my behavior to satisfy my critics, I leaned into the very things that seemed to make people upset, and Gina was right there by my side, leaning with me. We decided to launch our own line of cannabis vape pens designed for and marketed toward women. It was unlike anything else on the market.

The more Gina and I studied the cannabis market, the more it became clear that there was a specific demographic whose needs were being neglected, and it was one we were regularly serving. How was everyone else missing this? Well, it was possibly because it was the forgotten demographic in so many things: women.

As an OB-GYN, I've heard thousands of stories about the pain and issues that women have dealt with for years. These issues didn't go away when I stopped working as an OB-GYN; many women came to me at Greenhouse Wellness, hoping cannabis could give them relief.

Women have had a long, complicated relationship with medical science. It has recently come to light—or at least recently gotten more attention in the media—that women's pain and health concerns are often downplayed and undertreated by their health care professionals. There are so many stories about women being sent home with the dreaded "It's all in your head." In her 2018 book *Doing Harm*, Maya Dusenberry shared her discovery that women are more often dismissed and misdiagnosed than men, have to wait longer to receive care in the emergency room, and are 13–25 percent less likely to receive opioids when they say they're in pain.

It's no wonder that women can start to feel like they are "going crazy" or that their pain is in their heads and not worth treating. Just as it can be difficult to turn off all the noise and distraction and check back in with our beliefs and goals, it can be difficult to turn off all the doubt and outside chatter—especially when it comes from professionals in health care and wellness—and listen to what your body is telling you.

Traditional medicine has failed women for too long; maybe cannabis could offer a solution. Cannabis has been used specifically in women's health all over the globe for thousands of years. As women age, their complaints and medical problems change. Pain, anxiety, sexual dysfunction, hormonal imbalances, and sleep disturbances are pervasive. Our experience and research, as well as women's health studies, have revealed that women between twenty and forty commonly deal with acne, chronic pelvic pain, painful periods, endometriosis, sexual dysfunction, and premenstrual syndrome. Women over forty deal with sexual dysfunction, menopause symptoms (such as sleep problems and mood changes), and pain. Anxiety and sleep issues are the two most common ailments among our patients. Cannabis is particularly useful when it comes to treating those.

Now, if you don't mind a bit of science, I have a little more to share with you. Tetrahydrocannabinolic acid and terpenes enhance the effect of neurotransmitter gamma-aminobutyric acid, resulting in sedative, antianxiety, and muscle relaxant properties. CBD and terpenes also release serotonin in the brain, which improves overall mood. One of the natural endocannabinoids in our bodies is arachidonoylethanolamide, also called anandamide. Anandamide and estrogen levels are interactive, and a low estrogen level results in a lower level of anandamide in our bodies.

Another reason why medicinal cannabis is a wonderful therapeutic tool for women is because there are many cannabinoid receptors in the reproductive system, with a high concentration in the uterus, meaning cannabis relaxes uterine smooth muscle tissue and provides pain relief. Many of our basic reproductive functions are directly related to the endocannabinoid system, whether we are aware of it or not.

The endocannabinoid system in our bodies regulates our endocrine system, which regulates hormone production, metabolism, sexual function, sleep, mood, and more. The cannabinoids in cannabis interact with these systems directly, and the right formulation can provide tremendous relief.

Anandamide is involved in

- fertility, pregnancy, and reproductive systems;
- appetite;
- sex drive;
- sleep;
- motor control;
- inhibiting breast cancer cell proliferation;
- immune function;
- effects of other cannabinoids;
- temperature; and
- memory.

But its first-found benefit was how happy it could make people; this was one of the reasons it was called *anandamide*, derived from the Sanskrit word for bliss, *ananda*. This endocannabinoid's effects are mimicked by certain cannabinoids in cannabis, with certain combinations of them increasing or decreasing certain effects.

A recent survey distributed by *Eaze*—an online magazine devoted to cannabis use—found that women use cannabis as self-care, to reduce stress, and even to replace antidepressants and opioids.

．．．

All this information we learned about how cannabis can help women led us to conclude that it was high time there were cannabis products for women. It was those words *anandamide* and *bliss* that really struck us as we were brainstorming this line of products we wanted to create. Bliss is what we wanted for women, but we didn't want them to just be happier—we wanted them sleeping better, feeling less pain, and so much more. We wanted to create a product for all fierce ladies battling board meetings, managing families, and trying to live their best lives.

And that's when we came up with the concept for Blissiva. *Bliss + sativa* (which is, of course, a strain of cannabis) seemed to capture the idea we were going for. If you've ever looked at the names of cannabis strains out there, you know they can be distasteful and difficult to parse in terms of what you're getting. For example, "Pootie Tang" and "AK-47" are the actual names of strains you can buy—names, I might add, that are clearly marketed toward men. Though medical cannabis and CBD products in particular are becoming more mainstream, and some of the products themselves and their names are getting better, we didn't like the products we were seeing. They weren't attractive. They weren't well made. After doing all this research in cannabis and understanding how well wired a women's body is for cannabis, especially in the reproductive system and the uterus, we realized we could really do this.

Gina was hesitant to exclude 50 percent of our potential market right off the bat, and I understood where she was coming from. On the surface, it didn't necessarily seem like a good business move. But then we thought of all the cannabis products marketed toward men, and how we were just doing our part to at least *try* to level the playing field. We eventually agreed that marketing Blissiva to women was a good strategy. We imagined our sleek vape pen in its purple packaging would stand out among the more masculine-looking products, capturing the interest of women tired of browsing the same tired choices. Beyond that, Blissiva was a statement: Here is a product designed to satisfy women. It can satisfy men, too, but they weren't our target.

Sure, we were marketing toward only 50 percent of the populace, but we decided we would capture a higher percentage of that 50 than if we had marketed Blissiva more broadly. Soon after the release, one man came into Greenhouse Wellness and said, "You're just marketing this toward women." I'll never forget Kait's reaction: "And?"

Though our marketing strategy was clear, we by no means forbade men from trying Blissiva. In fact, 20 percent of our sales are from men who also want a discreet experience with a fabulous taste and inoffensive smell. Yes, we formulated it to address health concerns unique to women, but you don't need a vagina to buy it, and we're not so incredibly different that men can't enjoy its benefits too. One heavy THC user said Blissiva did wonders for his anxiety. Plenty of women buy products that are targeted toward men.

We sold out of product within six weeks. When we finally got more, people were walking out with bags full of vape pens, purchasing ten or more at a time. We got a call from a plastic surgeon who wanted to start recommending Blissiva instead of painkillers. We got more calls from people from across the country, asking when it would be available in their neck of the woods. In early April 2019, we announced a licensing agreement with the cannabis brand iAnthus, setting Blissiva on track to eventually reach women all over.

We were surprised and thrilled by the warm reception to Blissiva. Releasing it to the public and watching the reaction felt like a watershed moment for us. We were using it to stake a claim in the cannabis industry, as if to say, this isn't just one more industry for men to rule by default. Here's a product created by women and exclusively marketed toward women without a man's permission.

We're not done—not by a long shot. Cannabis has been used for thousands of years in women's health, and the medicine interacts with the female hormones and reproductive system through all stages of a woman's life. We have a product road map that encompasses all of the stages from puberty to menopause and everything in between.

The Blissiva manifesto is this:

- Don't settle. Don't look back and say, "I wish."
- Ask questions. Think through your own beliefs and goals, and question everything. Don't accept the normal viewpoint without thinking it through.
- Have a fresh perspective. The glass is neither half-full nor half-empty, but clearly, there is room for more wine.
- Push boundaries. Be disruptive.
- Don't take no for an answer. Sorry, not sorry.
- Be present—to work, life, and children.
- Be fearless. Showing up doesn't get you a ribbon. Losing teaches lessons.

Conclusion

Life should not be a journey to the grave
with the intention of arriving safely in a
pretty and well preserved body, but rather
to skid in broadside in a cloud of smoke,
thoroughly used up, totally worn out, and
loudly proclaiming, "Wow! What a Ride!"
—HUNTER THOMPSON

Gina and Leslie

We never thought we would own a dispensary. We never considered the idiosyncrasies involved in the cannabis space. But there was Gina, last summer, driving down the highway going to pick up a transfer of products from another dispensary. Summer day, windows down, country music playing, a cute little sequined purse with a pineapple on it. Just like every other suburban mother, right? Except that purse had 100 grams of shatter in it (and all the appropriate manifests). You just never know.

Our very first patient to enter the dispensary was incredibly motivated for us to open and had been emailing us for weeks before we officially had product available to sell. She had been injured in the service to our country and had hardware in her back after surgery to correct her spinal fractures. She was in constant pain, had a fentanyl pump, and was on a significant amount of oral morphine tablets. The opioids were ruining her life, and she was desperate to have help weaning off her pharmaceuticals. To get her off of her meds, we used a THC elixir, which she used to replace a dose of her oral pain meds. When she was off her morphine, she started to wean off the fentanyl pump. Within three months, she was off the opioids entirely, and she is now off the cannabis as well. She made such an impact on the whole staff—and especially on Leslie as a physician, who had never before seen the impact of cannabis on opioid use firsthand. We watched her personality change week to week, watched her change her gait as her pain lessened, and celebrated in unison when she announced she was off her pain meds completely. She changed everything for us. We watched in awe. Leslie isn't joking when she says, "This is the most impactful medicine I have ever practiced."

We keep a box of tissues handy at every station at our dispensary. We celebrate with those who succeed, commiserate with those who struggle, and grieve alongside the families of those we lose. We keep celebrating the good times and muddling through the bad: but we keep going. We had some amazing help and a bit of luck, but *we* did it. And you can too. Be unapologetic about saying no when you need to—say no until your tongue bleeds if that is what's right for you. And don't feel the need to explain why. Be yourself. Be true to who you are. Have a clear vision. That is the blueprint for success. Never take your eyes off the prize.

A lot of us live our lives inside the guardrails, but real change, real innovation, and real success all happen when we take risks. The biggest and best opportunities happen when there is disruption: the bigger the risk, the scarier it is, but it's the best chance for growth. Flex your muscles.

Now when we wake up in the morning, our first thought is often not "How did I get here?" but "How can we make the biggest impact today?" This is the career and the industry that we choose to remain in. We will stay, without any reservation, and continue to try to elevate every single element involved from the medicine to the business practices to the patient interactions and everything in between. We've accepted the downside, like the lost friends and the continued federal illegality. We still cry at the funerals of the patients who don't make it. But we cheer, too, because we think that cannabis is good medicine, and this is no longer a surprise to us. Leslie looks forward to an increase in robust studies on cannabis, providing information, the good and the bad, so physicians and providers can more confidently make safe treatment recommendations. Gina looks forward to the stigma going away so more people feel empowered to try cannabis without feeling ashamed or embarrassed. It's been a strange ride, to say the least, but as we embrace the next chapter in our adventure together. We echo Coco Chanel, who said, "Keep your heels, head, and standards high.".…. and for us, pun totally intended.

APPENDIX 1: COMMONLY ASKED QUESTIONS

From "5 Things I Wish Someone Told Me before I Started," *Authority Magazine*.

https://medium.com/authority-magazine/5-things-i-wish-someone-told-me-before-i-started-it-is-becoming-more-and-more-apparent-that-8f71acc81658

Can you share 3 things that most excite you about the Cannabis industry? Can you share 3 things that most concern you?

Exciting:

1. Seeing patients feel better in real time.

This is one that NEVER gets old. We have seen so many of our patients not only find relief from their physical symptoms, but many have also been able to wean themselves off of addictive opioid regimens. This is huge to us, as our nation battles a very intense opioid epidemic.

2. The receptivity to Blissiva.

As mothers and middle-aged women starting a dispensary, we certainly had our fair share of negative reactions. Certain friends of ours may not have understood (we never held it against them) and institutions like banks even took issue with us personally. However, seeing so many women (especially ones 50+) have SUCH a positive reaction to Blissiva validates our vision of making this medicine accessible to ALL by offering a safe and comfortable experience.

3. The stigma is certainly changing.

Again, even anecdotally, we could tell you this is happening as our patient base is largely comprised of baby boomers. We see parents coming in trying to find relief for their children (children who are 18+, of course) and even friends or family members (we have some relatives in law enforcement) who are changing their opinions and asking questions about how this medicine might bring relief to themselves or loved ones who are suffering. It's really encouraging to see the dialogue become much more inclusive and inquisitive versus just judgmental.

Concerning:

1. Big business coming in.

We bid in two other states after winning a license in Maryland (Pennsylvania and Ohio), and it has become very clear that already in this burgeoning stage of the industry, consolidation and big business are taking a lead. Even in Pennsylvania, where the state opened up the application process again, nearly all those who won in the second round were large, multi-state companies. This is concerning because it's really edging out the ability for smaller, independent businesses with deep ties to their communities to thrive.

2. Monopolies.

The big companies are positioning themselves to monopolize the market, and this will limit the options that are available to patients as far as what medicines are available, as sadly, the large companies answer to their shareholders and profit over patients.

3. Unintended consequences of the plant becoming recreationally legal.

Also concerning is the unintended consequences of the plant becoming recreationally legal. When this happens, the trends indicate that versions of the plant that are very medically focused (i.e.

higher CBD amounts) aren't as accessible because the recreational demand is more focused on high THC products. While we certainly hold no judgment around that desire, those products are not always the best for those whose intention is medical, not recreational, in nature.

Can you share your "5 Things I Wish Someone Told Me before I Started Leading a Cannabis Business"? Please share a story or example for each.

1. You'll lose friends.

Some folks just can't accept cannabis as an alternative healing method, and can't even agree to disagree because their "just say no" to drugs mentality is so hardwired. We hope that with the tincture of time, their opinions will change as more and more data become available on the validity of cannabis as a medicine and that the friendships will return.

2. You'll lose a bank.

Gina's personal bank, who she'd done business with for 35 years, saw in the paper that she won the medical cannabis dispensary bid—which was in her personal name, as we hadn't had time to create an LLC or anything—and "invited her" to remove all her accounts from the bank. Basically, her personal bank tried to cancel her personal account. They had their mortgages there, all of their family's checking accounts, the kids' savings accounts—it was a cold slap in the face, and one of the first experiences we had of feeling like "pariahs."

3. It's harder than any other business.

We have found that in this industry, there are a lot of cannabis enthusiasts who saw a business opportunity, and perhaps not as many business enthusiasts who saw a cannabis opportunity. That can be challenging for some, because at the end of the day, in our case, you are running a retail business, which can be difficult. You have to deal with part-time employees, inventory management, supply and demand, and more. We are business enthusiasts, so we manage these things fairly well, but they are still challenging.

4. Cannabis is really impactful medicine.

Had I known how impactful this medicine would be, I would have wanted to jump in sooner, and I would have focused on educating others much earlier. There is so much opportunity around cannabis education, and my role these days is really to educate those around me, from the patients, to the community, to the medical practitioners. There is so much to learn, and the potential for healing from cannabis is so great that we have just scratched the surface. I am excited to see what comes next.

5. How big business would come in and snatch everything up.

It is becoming more and more apparent that smaller businesses are being edged out. With the large, multi-state companies buying up the smaller licenses, those with passion for providing patients with quality and safe medical cannabis options will no longer have a voice. In the bidding war for new licenses, the large companies are edging out the smaller independents, as they have much deeper pockets to buy their way in. Also, because they control so much of the market, they can sell to themselves at lower price points than the independents can buy it wholesale, which puts undue economic pressures on the smaller companies and can force them out of business.

What advice would you give to other CEOs or founders to help their employees to thrive?

Definitely implement a training program. Product knowledge and customer experience is key to maintaining a great brand and growing patient base. The more you educate your employees and the better you treat them, the more this will reflect in their interactions with patients, and all will benefit.

Additionally, always emphasize what makes you different. We were nervous about being one of the only women-owned cannabis businesses in the state and taking such a strong medical approach when many of our competitors were positioning themselves more recreationally, but this made us stand out. We'd find patients who would drive, in some cases a couple hours, just for that unique difference.

You are a person of great influence. If you could inspire a movement that would bring the most amount of good to the most

amount of people, what would that be? You never know what your idea can trigger. :-)

Definitely inspiring more women in business. We are currently in the process of writing a book about how we founded Greenhouse Wellness and Blissiva, and the true intention behind this endeavor is to encourage other women to unapologetically "go for it." We were two working mothers with many odds stacked against us—we were in an industry we knew nothing about at the time, one that was heavily stigmatized, and one that had very few women in it—and we just went for it and didn't look back. While the number of stories of female entrepreneurs are certainly increasing, we still have a long way to go in providing examples that let other women know it's okay to throw your hat in the ring.

We hope our story will serve as an inspiration and a love letter—for other women who are forging their own ways in their careers and lives, becoming their own types of disruptors, and challenging the status quo. It's certainly the mantra we go to bed with, and we hope it'll be the fight song other women wake up to, or the pat on the back when they are doubting themselves.

What is the best way our readers can follow you on social media?
Instagram:
@blissiva—https://www.instagram.com/blissiva/
@greenhousewellnessmd — https://www.instagram.com/greenhousewellnessmd/
Facebook:
https://www.facebook.com/greenhousewellness
https://www.facebook.com/Blissiva-1048898915277342/

APPENDIX 2: QUICK OVERVIEW OF CANNABIS

Cannabis has been used for thousands of years all over the world. The plant is thought to have originated in what is now Kazakhstan, about fifty million years ago. The very high concentration of cannabinoids in the plant may have evolved to help protect the plant from harmful UV rays due to the high altitude or as a deterrent against being consumed by local fauna. The fact that so many creatures on the planet also evolved a primitive nervous system with receptors for these phyto-cannabinoids (plant-based cannabinoids) is certainly fascinating, and wild cannabis or hemp flourished in the outskirts of early human settlements for thousands of years.

Cannabis and hemp are genetically identical but have been manipulated by humans to be quite different today. By definition, hemp is cannabis that contains less than 0.3 percent THC. Original wild cannabis probably had around 3–5 percent THC and had higher amounts of CBD, or cannabidiol, the other major cannabinoid found in cannabis. CBD is nonintoxicating and can actually protect the user from the annoying side effects of THC, which can include dizziness, anxiety, paranoia, and agitation. CBD is a powerful anti-inflammatory. It is absolutely everywhere these days, thanks to the farm bill, and many think CBD will be a bigger market than cannabis itself.

There are hundreds of cannabinoids and other compounds in cannabis. A staggering amount of interplay happens between all of them to give the user an augmented effect known as the entourage effect. This means that the total effect is greater than the sum of its parts. Cannabigerolic acid (CBGa) is the mother molecule from which the other cannabinoids are derived. The *a* means *acid group*. When you see a cannabinoid with an *a* on your product label, it means the product hasn't been heated or treated to remove the CO_2 group. THCa, for example, does not induce a high, but it is incredibly helpful for pain and anxiety. We look for products that contain the acid forms, as they are so helpful when treating certain medical conditions.

When heated (smoked, vaped, or processed), the acid groups are removed from their cannabinoids, which changes the way they affect the body. Delta 9 THC, which is the form you get when smoking or vaping, affects the body quite differently than 11-OH THC, which is the form you get after ingesting THC orally. 11-OH THC is ten times more potent than delta 9 THC and will last in the body a lot longer, so when a doctor is treating patients with chronic pain, it makes sense for the patients to ingest the medicine orally rather than smoke or vape it. There is also delta 8 THC, which gives a softer, shorter-lived effect. THCv is of great interest to many, as it can suppress appetite and has been useful in treating obesity and diabetes. Based on the studies we do have, it looks like most of the components of cannabis are antioxidants and/or anti-inflammatory. Many are antibacterial and antifungal. Some have been shown to specifically target and kill cancer cells while sparing normal cells. Further, they can interfere with cancer's ability to metastasize and also prevent the growth of new blood vessels around tumors. While this is all incredibly exciting, we will wait for traditional medicine to catch up with robust studies and trials before announcing that cannabis cures all. The legitimization of cannabis as medicine will allow for the full potential of the plant to be recognized eventually.

Terpenes are another fascinating component in cannabis, and we have all been exposed to them and ingesting them our whole lives unknowingly. Terpenes exist in cannabis but also in many other plants. Linalool is in lavender and is useful in treating seizures, inducing sleep, and calming anxiety. Limonene is in citrus fruits and is uplifting, helps anxiety, and is rejuvenating. Pinene, also in pine needles, is a bronchodilator and is quite calming. Myrcene, also in hops and mango, helps to strengthen the effects of the cannabinoids in the body and is helpful in sleep disorders. There are too many others to mention, but terpenes are the components of the plant that direct traffic, so to speak. They affect the cannabinoids differently and determine their effects on our bodies. When our patients find a combination of cannabinoids with the right ratios of terpenes, they know instantly that they are on to something. Everyone's body reacts a bit differently to the exact same compounds, so one size might not fit all. As in all aspects of medicine, the user needs to start low, go slowly, and experiment until the right mixture is determined. As in traditional medicine, if a patient is started on one kind of blood pressure medicine, they are asked to return in a few weeks to ensure it is working and that they are not having unwanted side effects. Sometimes, dosages need to be adjusted, or another kind of medicine is tried instead. Trial and error. Cannabis medicine is no different.

All parts of the plant are useful. The stalk can be made into ropes and cloth and can be used as food for livestock and humans, and the seeds are almost a complete food source. That means that one could live almost entirely on hemp seeds and receive the necessary amino acids and proteins to survive long term. The plant is also used to make medicines, tonics, and salves and in cosmetics and shampoos. The sky is the limit when it comes to cannabis. For this reason, it was mandated in the original thirteen colonies that every homeowner grow their own hemp crop for harvest.

Cannabis was added to the *US Pharmacopeia* in 1850 as a medical treatment option, but when aspirin and morphine tablets were introduced, the more reproducible dosing of a tablet was preferable to the unpredictability of cannabis tinctures, especially as processing and testing techniques had not yet been perfected. Due to a sequence of fairly insane historical and political events, cannabis was removed from traditional medicine and deemed of no value in the early 1900s. In 1970 came the final blow, when cannabis was labeled a Schedule 1 drug—the same category as heroin, ecstasy, and LSD. These drugs are deemed to have no medical value, their safety profile cannot be established, and they have a high potential for abuse. Funny enough, the government has owned the patent for cannabinoids as antioxidants and neuroprotectants since 2003. Seems a bit contradictory given the definition of cannabis as a Schedule 1 drug.

How sad that thousands of years of experience went down the drain and cannabis was no longer legally available after 1970. That didn't stop humans from continuing to cultivate the plant behind the scenes, however. And they bred their cannabis to be ever stronger and contain more and more THC, which is the intoxicating cannabinoid. Because of the illegal nature, smoking was really the only way mainstream Americans could access this medicine, and the negative stigma associated with all of this persists to this day. Happily, that is changing, and now that other countries have legalized cannabis, we are seeing more and more robust studies in the literature. Given that as of the time of this printing, thirty-three states now have a medical or legal program, we see the writing on the wall. We anticipate national legalization soon. While we both think this is the right course, we are concerned about the continued push for higher and higher THC plants without the focus on CBD-rich alternatives. Legalization is fine, but our continued wish is that the cannabis industry embraces and learns from what science and good data provide over the next few years. As we get more sophisticated in our processing and testing, and as we get more knowledge about our own endocannabinoid system and the major and minor cannabinoids, we look forward to better customization of products and strains to treat the specific ailments of our patients in the best way possible. That is our goal. That is our focus. That is Blissiva.

These days, one can find multiple different formulations of cannabis. It turns out that the method by which one consumes the medicine has a huge impact on how it works. Salves and rubs applied topically don't get absorbed into the bloodstream, so the patient gets excellent pain relief but doesn't get the cerebral high. There are bath oils and salts to add to your tub so you can soak your troubles away. There are even patches that can be placed inconspicuously that afford the user up to twenty-four hours of relief.

There are drinks, tablets, chewables, tinctures, and more that give long-lasting benefits, but when someone is in real trouble, whether suffering from pain, anxiety, migraine aura, or other, the fact that vaping or smoking will bring about almost instantaneous relief is a godsend.

States that have legalized cannabis have seen a 25 percent drop in opioid-related deaths. This drop doesn't fade away after time but *strengthens*. It appears that cannabis is saving lives, not claiming them, as the prohibitionists would have liked us to believe. The reason for this is that there are very few receptors for cannabis in the brain stem, so it is impossible to overdose on cannabis, as can happen with opioids and alcohol. Cannabis, by itself, cannot kill you, but it can certainly make you do stupid things—like drive while impaired or make other unintelligent choices. The fact that cannabis is being used to help those on opioids wean off and reclaim their lives is a real breath of fresh air these days. Cannabis still has a long way to go to overcome the stigmas of the past, but each patient who comes into the dispensary with a smile that goes from ear to ear and announces, "I'm off all my meds!" gives us reason to fight harder every tomorrow.

The science of cannabis can be intimidating, as many of us did not grow up being exposed to these terms. We encourage you to dive a little deeper if you are interested in cannabis as medicine. There are many great resources for you to use. Here are some of our favorites:

Medical Marijuana Guide, by Patricia Frye, MD, with Dave Smitherman

Cannabis Pharmacy, by Michael Backes

NO LONGER PROPERTY OF
SEATTLE PUBLIC LIBRARY

CPSIA information can be obtained
at www.ICGtesting.com
Printed in the USA
LVHW021634020220
645577LV00011B/968

9 781733 226707